Augustine's *Confessions*

LIVES OF GREAT RELIGIOUS BOOKS

The Tibetan Book of the Dead, Donald S. Lopez, Jr.

Dietrich Bonhoeffer's *Letters and Papers from Prison*, Martin E. Marty

Augustine's *Confessions*, Garry Wills

FORTHCOMING:

Revelation, Bruce Chilton

The Analects of Confucius, Annping Chin and Jonathan D. Spence

The Dead Sea Scrolls, John J. Collins

The Bhagavad Gita, Richard H. Davis

Josephus's *The Jewish War,* Martin Goodman

The Book of Mormon, Paul Gutjahr

The Book of Genesis, Ronald S. Hendel

The Book of Job, Mark Larrimore

The Greatest Translations of All Time: *The Septuagint* and *The Vulgate,* Jack Miles

The Passover Haggadah, Vanessa Ochs

The Song of Songs, Ilana Pardes

Rumi's *Masnavi*, Omid Safi

The I Ching, Richard J. Smith

The Yoga Sutras of Patanjali, David Gordon White

Augustine's *Confessions*

A BIOGRAPHY

Garry Wills

PRINCETON UNIVERSITY PRESS

Princeton and Oxford

Jacket illustration: *Vision of Saint Augustine*, by Vittore Carpaccio (1455–1525). Photo: Mauro Magliani, 1998; courtesy of Alinari / Art Resource, NY

Library of Congress Cataloging-in-Publication Data

Wills, Garry, 1934–

    Augustine's Confessions : a biography / Garry Wills.

        p. cm. — (Lives of great religious books)

    Includes bibliographical references (p.) and index.

    ISBN 978-0-691-14357-6 (hardcover : alk. paper)

    1. Augustine, Saint, Bishop of Hippo. Confessiones.   2. Christian saints—Algeria—Hippo (Extinct city)—Biography—History and criticism.   I. Title.

    BR65.A62W55 2011

    270.2092—dc22   2010016452

British Library Cataloging-in-Publication Data is available

This book has been composed in Garamond Premier Pro

Printed on acid-free paper. ∞

Printed in the United States of America

10 9 8 7 6 5 4 3 2 1

CONTENTS

A Note on the Translation   vii

CHAPTER 1   The Book's Birth   1

CHAPTER 2   The Book's Genre   17

CHAPTER 3   The Book's African Days   26

CHAPTER 4   The Book's Ambrose   41

CHAPTER 5   The Book's "Conversion"   58

CHAPTER 6   The Book's Baptismal Days   78

CHAPTER 7   The Book's Hinge   98

CHAPTER 8   The Book's Culmination   112

CHAPTER 9   The Book's Afterlife: *Early Reception, Later Neglect*   133

NOTES   149

BASIC READINGS   155

INDEX   157

A NOTE ON THE TRANSLATIONS

All translations are by the author. Those from the Bible are given according to Augustine's Latin citations of it.

References to O'Donnell are to volume and page of James J. O'Donnell, *Augustine "Confessions,"* 3 vols. (Oxford University Press, 1992).

Augustine's *Confessions*

The Book's Birth

To write the biography of *Confessions*, we have to start in the delivery room—how and when was it born? We shall see that the when can partly be determined by the how. How did Augustine write *Confessions*? Well, in the strict sense, he didn't— didn't set words down on papyrus or parchment. Augustine has been painted, by artists as great as Botticelli, Carpaccio, and Benozzo Gozzoli, seated at a desk and writing. He did not do that. Oh, he undoubtedly wrote things like notes to himself, or lists of items, or instructions to individual brothers in his monastic community. But the books, sermons, and letters that have come down to us were all dictated to scribes. Even a book that feels as intimate as *Confessions* was spoken to several of the many scribes Augustine kept busy. That was the normal practice in antiquity. Even in prison, Saint Paul had a scribe on hand. Even when living as a hermit, Saint Jerome had teams of scribes. The population of ancient scribes was a vast one.

Writing was a complex and clumsy process. That was especially true in the classical period, when papyrus scrolls were used. One needed at least three hands to unroll the scroll on the left, to roll it up on the right, and to write a series of columns in the intermediate spaces. Besides, even the mixing of the ink and trimming of the reed pens (quills arrived in the Middle Ages) had to be done while the scroll was held open at the spot reached by the scribe. Since the rolls were written on one side only, they could run to great lengths, as much as thirty feet long.

Obviously, the author could not be doing all this and composing in his mind. The only efficient way to function was for the author to dictate to a shorthand writer (tachygrapher), who took the text down on tablets of wax or wood. Then this first scribe, with the help of assistants, would write the text on a scroll. Other scribes would copy this text on other scrolls—the only way to duplicate a text in the age before printing presses. A man would read slowly from the master text while a number of scribes created their own copies. There was no need for these secondary scribes to decipher the first man's shorthand signs. After he made the master copy, multiple facsimiles were needed. Paul sent copies of the same letter to several places—to the churches of Galatia for instance. He sent his Epistle to the Romans to Jerusalem as well as to Rome. He also had to keep copies by him, for his own reference and to supply those asking for clarification of the record.

Writings, created with such labor, could be lost in transit where couriers were careless or in peril—Augustine's first letter sent to Jerome did not reach him, causing endless later trouble. Books could easily disappear if there were not enough copies made or preserved. Even though Augustine kept his own archives in good order, his very first book is irretrievably lost. Teams of scribes had to be kept at work all the time to bring a book into existence and keep it there. The Late Antique church historian Eusebius tells us that the church father Origen had seven tachygraphers and a horde of other scribes and calligraphers to replicate what the shorthand experts took down and wrote out (*History of the Church* 6.23).

The making of books was an expensive as well as laborious and time-consuming process. One of the principal costs of Augustine's episcopal establishment was the production of his many books. He wrote five million words that have come down to us, most of them after he became the bishop of Hippo. Isidore of Seville famously said that anyone who claims to have read all of Augustine must be a liar. In a recently discovered letter (Divjak 23-A), Augustine says that in less than three months he had dictated 6,000 lines of text—James O'Donnell suggests he made the count for payment to his scribes.

Besides all the scribal payments, there was the costly material of which books were made. To form double-ply sheets from the papyrus plant was labor-intensive, from cutting to cross-laying to drying. Even more difficult was the skinning, stretching, scraping, and drying of sheep or calf or goat skin to make parchment. And copyists had to keep the sheet numbers in order if they wrote the text before the sheaves (quires) were bound into a codex. Augustine had to be serviced by what amounts to a literary industrial complex in order to produce the amazing number of his books.

It may distance Augustine from us if we think we are not communing with him directly as he writes in solitude, just as we read in solitude. But this is the exact reverse of the ancients' view. Theirs was an oral culture; they learned better and remembered ✓ better when they heard words sounded by a human voice. Plato makes Socrates say that spoken discourse pierces to the soul, while writing lies on the surface (*Phaedrus* 276b–d). Ancient readers did not normally read in solitude. As writing was a cumbrous process, reading was a clumsy one. People most often read aloud, even when they were alone. Augustine says that it puzzled people to see Ambrose reading silently (*Confessions* 6.3). Reading was difficult, since the letters were written without word-separation or punctuation (*scripta continua*). When Paul sent a letter to a gathering, an official *lector* read it aloud—most in the gathering were not able to make sense of the written row of letters. That is why the author of Revelation says, "Happy whoever reads these words out, and happy those who hear him" (1.3).

So even written words were shot through with oral elements—the vocal phenomena of the author at one end of the process dictating and a reader at the other end voicing the words. The writing was almost like a musical score—a set of signs to be given acoustical reality in performance. For Augustine's contemporaries, this "bypassing" of the merely written would make his words all the more vivid. Paul hints at such bypassing of the written when he says to the Corinthians,

> Am I renewing my introduction to you—do I, like others, really need (or don't I) credentials presented to you or by you? Yourselves are my credentials, written on my heart—there all can find and read them. You are in fact a letter sent by Messiah for me to deliver, one not written in ink but in the Spirit of the living God, written not on stone tablets but on the fleshy tablets of the heart. (2 Cor. 3.1)

There are other ways writing was made to serve oral delivery. In Ezekiel's vision, a hand reaches down from heaven with a scroll in it. "Man, eat what is in front of you, eat this scroll, *and then go and speak to the Israelites*" (Ezek. 3.1). The prophet digests the divine message so he can *speak* it. Similarly, the prophet in Revelation (10.10–11) swallows the "little scroll" in the angel's hand, and the angel tells him to go prophesy. So, paradoxically, the oral externals of Augustine's performance convey more inwardness to his original audience than writing alone could do.

The difficulty of reading in the ancient world had another impact on *Confessions*. The *scripta continua*, with no word divisions, no chapter-and-verse markings, made it hard to look up citations in a scroll or codex Since Augustine weaves a constant web of scriptural language throughout his text, it is clear that he is relying principally on his capacious memory in these citations—not looking them up, one by one. The power of memory in an oral culture is proverbial. Thomas Jefferson, who thought black people intellectually inferior to whites, marveled at their memory, a side-product of their oral culture (*Notes on the State of Virginia*, Query XIV). Cicero said that all public speakers must have well-trained memories (*The Orator* 2.350–60). The ancient orators did not read speeches to their audience (a difficult process, whether with scroll or codex), but memorized long orations—something still possible in the nineteenth century, when Edward Everett delivered his two-hour address at Gettysburg from memory (his regular practice when speaking on solemn occasions). Augustine, as we shall see, explored the vast capabilities of memory in *Confessions* Book 10. He was an example of what he is analyzing and praising there. His intimate knowledge of Scripture was necessary to his performance of *Confessions*.

The fact that Augustine cited Scripture from memory explains his resistance to the new translation Jerome was making into Latin of the Jewish Scripture from the Hebrew original rather than from the Greek translation (Septuagint). Augustine, who only spoke Latin, had memorized his Bible in the Latin translation familiar in Africa. It was a wrench to jettison that hard-won memorization of so large a body of work. (See Augustine, *Letters* 28.2, 71.3–6, 82.34–35). The familiar Latin words had become a part of Augustine, one he did not want to disturb unduly.

Augustine, like Ezekiel, or like the John of Revelation, had "eaten" the Scripture and afterward thought in its terms and rhythms, with and through its words. It is sometimes said that authors like Abraham Lincoln were so influenced by the King James English Bible that it affected their style. But the omnipresence of Scripture in Augustine goes far beyond that. Scripture informs the whole long prayer that is *Confessions*. The echoes are not footnoted or underlined in the original, but italics here will suggest how deeply interfused are Augustine's words and the Bible's:

> To whom before you should I call out, *Cleanse me of my inmost sins, and outward promptings fend off from your servant*? I believe in you and that is why, you know Lord, I address you. Have I not anticipated accusation of my own sins, and *you freed my heart of impiety*? I do not *take you into court*, you who are Truth. I would not deceive myself, not let

CHAPTER I

my *iniquity tell itself a lie*, so I *go not to court* with you. *If you arraign our sins, Lord—Lord, who can stand the indictment ?* (1.6)

The sacred writings are present in *Confessions* not only when Augustine quotes them but in the way he uses his own words. The most basic verse structure of the Psalms, as of all Hebrew poetry, is a two-line unit in which the second line repeats, reverses, or elaborates on the first one. An example is quoted in the opening words of *Confessions,* from Psalm 146.5:

Vast is what you do,
    what you know beyond assaying.

This pattern informs much of *Confessions*, its sighing replications, his way of turning a thought over and over. These give the book its air of slow reflection and inwardness. The words cast a spell and we are taken down into Augustine's deepest self. Thus, by a paradox, Augustine's use of other people's words (the sacred authors') helps him speak most authentically as himself.

The fact that Augustine can maintain this meditative spell in *Confessions* is a key to its dating. Once launched on this interior exploration, Augustine sustains a tone and intensity throughout at least the first ten books (we can argue later about the last three). It is true that Augustine composed some works over a number of years—notably *City of God* and *The Trinity.* But *City of God* is a work whose purpose and method shifted over the years of its composition, and work on *The Trinity* was suspended because of an accident—and those books do not have the incantatory continuity of *Confessions.* A sustained single effort seems to have produced *Confessions.*

This has been doubted by some. The book must have been begun in 397, before Augustine learned of Ambrose's death in that year, since there is no awareness that he has died. But Augustine stops the narrative part of the book at Book 9, the time of his baptism ten years earlier. Yet Book 10 gives an account of his soul at the time of writing. Some think that the first nine books were released by themselves, and readers asked what his state was after that decade. They point to a passage of Book 10 that says:

> The testimony to my past sins—which you have forgiven and hidden away to give me happiness in you, transforming my soul by faith and by baptism into you—may that testimony stir the heart in those who read or hear it. (10.4)

That does not say people have read some *earlier form* of the present work. It is more natural to think they have been reading the present text, the one he is continuing. The matter is clearer in the passage that is most often used to claim that Book 10 was not an original part of *Confessions*:

> Many have asked what my condition is at the moment of my testifying, both those who know me and those who know me not but have heard something from me or about me. (10)

He does not say some people have read the earlier parts of this book, or that they have necessarily read anything. He refers to those have *heard (audierunt) something (aliquid)* from me or about me (*ex me vel de me*). Nothing could be more general, more non-specific about *Confessions* or any other book. If he is being asked by those who know him personally, that does not restrict the questions to anything that has been written by him or about him. And those who have only heard "about me," contrasted with those who have heard "from me," are getting their information from someone else, not from *Confessions*.

Who was likely to ask these questions? If they were people who had read an earlier version of *Confessions*, the more expected request would be that he continue the story, not that he would break off and make a later report. Who, by contrast, would be likely to ask that he give an account of himself in 397? There were many who challenged Augustine, not only foes like the Manicheans or Donatists, but those of his own faith who (as we shall see) questioned the validity of his consecration as bishop or had heard other rumors. The occasion of questioning was, therefore, not obviously the reading of Books 1 through 9 in an earlier published form.

Nonetheless, for a long time many scholars thought Book 10 was added later on. They then went on to ask when the book was added. They settled on 401 because of some verbal similarities between Book 10 and *Explaining the Psalms*, Psalm 36, which was dated to 401. But if Augustine was partly repeating himself, would he do it at the same time, or later? The latter seems more likely, as occasion arose. Besides, Pierre-Marie Hombert has dated the psalm commentary to 403, stretching the composition of *Confessions* to six years (397–403).[1]

Some who would not date Book 10 after the first nine books do think that Books 11–13 were added later. After all, even Book 10 is about Augustine, while the last three books are outside the narrative of *Confessions* entirely. They are an exegetical exercise on the opening of Genesis. To some they seem so outside the ambit of the book that they are rarely read, and some earlier translations omitted them. Which raises an important point: if these books are so disjunct from the rest of *Confessions*, why did Augustine tack them on, either originally or at some later point?

But Genesis is present all through the book. Episodes in Genesis lie behind key events in Augustine's life, as we shall see. The God who made the world is still remaking Augustine by his secret providence and graces. Furthermore, Augustine finds the mystery of the Trinity implicit in the creation story, and the Trinity has also been haunting the entire book. James O'Donnell has traced the way patterns of three are everywhere in *Confessions*. It is clear that Augustine had Books 11 through 13 in mind as he steered the book toward its culmination. This also gives a special meaning to Book 10. Augustine purifies himself there as a preparation for plunging deep into the sacred writings of Scripture. It is like the examination of conscience (Confiteor) before beginning the Mass. Or like the meditation on death and judgment at the west entrance to a medieval cathedral.

Confessions is written as a deliberate whole. If it was added to after 397, why is there no belated notice of Ambrose's death? Of course, some items may have pre-existed the finished book and been worked into its texture, including the tribute to his mother in Book 9 (written perhaps at her death in 387) and the mini-biography of Alypius in Book 6 (written perhaps when he was consecrated bishop around 395).

For much of his other work, Augustine had to dictate in the times he could snatch away from his duties as a bishop who was constantly preaching and counseling. How did he find a chunk of relatively free time to dictate the *Confessions* in one go? Oddly, he may have been forced to spend time immobilized by a debilitating ailment. It was in 397 that he wrote to a fellow bishop, Profuturus:

> In regard to the spirit, as God allows, and as he grants me endurance, I am doing well. But in regard to the body, I am confined to bed, unable to walk or stand or sit, from the pain and swelling of anal fissures and hemorrhoids. But since God allows this, what can I say but that I am doing well? If our will does not conform to his will, we are at fault, since he is not to be thought of as doing or allowing anything that is not for our good. You know this, but since you are my second self, why should I not say as freely to you what I say to myself? So I trust my days and nights to your holy prayers. Pray that I do not use the days

wastefully, and that I bear the nights with compo-
sure. (Letter 38.1)

It seems likely that *Confessions* was delivered
from birth throes indeed, emerging from this combination of pain, serenity, and prayer. He was surely
not "using his days wastefully." The obstetric record
of *Confessions* can thus be briefly stated. It was born
in Hippo, Africa, by a prolonged bout of dictation
in the year 397 CE, when Augustine was forty-three
years old, ten years after his baptism, six years after
his ordination as a priest, and a little over a year
after his consecration as a bishop.

The biography of a person begins with the person's heritage and birth, then plots his or her development over the course of the life (*bios*), ending at
the person's death (*thanatos*), tracing connections,
arguing with misperceptions about the life, empha-
sizing what was most significant about the person.
Similarly, the biography of a book should describe
its internal development, what makes it work, what
challenges it meets. But a book, if it is a good and
important one, does not die as a person does. The
person has a later reputation, to be attacked or de-
fended, interpreted and reinterpreted. But a book
can be read and experienced after it is finished, just
as it was when it was written. It has an afterlife

(*Nachleben*, as the Germans say) that is different from a person's.

Confessions did have a kind of death, during the greater part of the Middle Ages, when it was (comparatively) neglected while clerics paid more attention to Augustine's doctrinal works. But *Confessions* had a kind of resurrection in the fourteenth century, when medieval myths and legends and supposed miracles overshadowed his own account of his life. After that there were waves of new interpretations of the book—textual in the Renaissance, romantic in the eighteenth century, historiographical in the nineteenth century, psychological in the twentieth century, post-structural in the twenty-first century. Many of these interpretations were misinterpretations, which I anticipate in telling the story of the book in the first place—dealing with the problem of the book's unity, with its departure from Augustine's own earlier accounts, with key relations (to his mother, to Ambrose and Simplician, to Faustus and Mallius Theodore). Since much of the debate during the book's *Nachleben* has been dealt with in the biography of the book itself, the last chapter can be summary, reflecting back on the course of the book as first defined.

The Book's Genre

CHAPTER 2

Augustine had never written anything like *Confessions*. In fact, no one had ever written anything like this book. James O'Donnell (2.8) points out that its very opening has no parallel in classical or Christian literature: "No other work of his begins with direct address to God.... Augustine invented a form and style unique in his own oeuvre and in the traditions he inherited." How did his other work lead to this odd product?

His writing career was at this point uneven. He wrote only one book before the age of thirty-two, *The Beautiful and the Decorous*, a lost work he called a show-off piece and sent to a celebrity rhetorician, hoping to attract his attention. (It didn't.) But then, when he prepared for baptism in 386, there was a spurt of dialogues recording discussion with his friends, students, and mother. At this point Augustine planned a cycle of works on the liberal arts seen from a Christian perspective. Only one of these books, *Music*, was completed. When he went back to his birthplace in Africa, he was caught up in controversy with his former fellows in the Manichean movement. It was partly because he was seen as a champion against these dissidents that he was dragooned into the priesthood in 291 (public demand was the normal path to ordination then).

Though Augustine was popular enough in the town where he became a priest, Hippo, to be further recruited as a bishop four years later, his identity was not firmly established outside his immediate flock. For all his early adult life in Africa he had been a Manichean, an active proselytizer of that faith throughout his twenties. He went off to Italy under Manichean patronage when he was twenty-nine, and returned four years later, after baptism in Milan, as the member of a new faith. But what was that faith? It is not enough to call him a Christian, since Manicheans were Christians (but of a heretical sort). The majority Christian faith in Africa at the time was Donatist, a purist body that had resisted the Emperor Diocletian's persecution at the beginning of the fourth century. These purists accused other Christians of collaboration with the persecutors. These laxer sorts were associated with Bishop Caecilian, so some historians call the minority Christian body in Africa Caecilianists. That was the faction Augustine joined, though members of his family had been Donatists (including his mother), and some still were.

How was Augustine, a member of the minority Christian branch with compromising past ties to Donatists and Manicheans, to distinguish his own religious stance? It was not enough to argue with Manicheans, who claimed he was a turncoat. There was also a problem with his consecration as a bishop. Augustine had left his hometown to recruit a man in Hippo. Traveling could be dangerous when communities could appoint a man a priest against his will. That is what happened to Augustine in Hippo, a modest town of perhaps 30,000 people, one tenth the size of Carthage, Africa's leading city. Once Augustine became a popular preacher in Hippo, the bishop there, Valerius, came to rely on his services, since Valerius was a native Greek speaker with shaky Latin. It was against the canons of the African church for a bishop to allow a priest to preach in his own church, but Valerius not only did this—he hid Augustine from visiting clerics, lest he be spirited away to a more flourishing environment.

Valerius wanted to keep Augustine in his dim place, and there was only one way to do that. A priest could always leave a town, but a bishop could never leave his community. He was "married" to it for life. So Valerius made Augustine his associate bishop. The problem here is that the Council of Nicaea had decreed there could be only one bishop in a community. Accusations of irregularity would haunt Augustine even after Valerius died, a year after consecrating Augustine.

There were, therefore, many reasons for Augustine to establish his identity in his new office as bishop. He had become a Christian in far-off Milan, in circumstances few in Africa could know about until he explained them. This leads some students of Augustine to think of *Confessions* as a defence of an embattled figure, much like John Henry Newman's *Apologia pro Vita Sua* or the *Apologia* Plato puts in the mouth of Socrates. But Augustine had other things in mind, too. He had reached a stage where he wanted to define his role in a new way. Bishops in the Africa of his time were rarely great preachers and never great theologians. Augustine now wanted to be a philosopher-bishop, of a type he had encountered in Ambrose at Milan, but one that was a novelty in his home country. To this point he had had little time to do serious immersion in Scripture. He had to change the rhythms of his life. *Confessions* was a kind of retreat into himself, to prepare himself for the ambitious theological works coming up—*The Trinity*, especially, and *First Meanings in Genesis*.

The first thing that sets *Confessions* apart from books like Newman's *Apologia* is its audience. He addresses himself to only one hearer, God. The whole book is one long prayer, perhaps the longest literary prayer among the great books of the West. As James O'Donnell says,

> He gestures in our direction and mentions us from time to time, but he *never addresses his readers*. As literary text, *Confession*s resembles a one-sided, non-fiction epistolary novel, enacted in the presence of the silence (and darkness) of God. What he attempts is a radical turn away from common sense—seen as tragically flawed by mad self-love—towards the wholly other, and thus toward the true self—for to him, we are not who we think we are. (2.9)

The prayer genre sets this book apart from other self-examinations, including Augustine's early *Dialogues With Myself (Soliloquia)* or the *To Myself* of Marcus Aurelius (most often translated as *Meditations*). There the author is speaking to himself, not to God.

Confessions is commonly read as an autobiography—some even call it the first autobiography. It does not fit into that genre. God does not need to learn anything about Augustine's life. Augustine is trying to acknowledge the graces that make his life part of sacred history—whence the constant use of Scripture. Things that we expect, or even demand, from autobiography are missing here. We learn nothing about Augustine's sister, almost nothing about his brother. The names of his best friend and his common-law wife are never given us, nor is the name of Mallius Theodore, the man he attributed his conversion to at the time (*Happiness in This Life* 1). We are not told of his dealings with the emperor whose court he graced in Milan, or of the Christian communities he met with in Rome and Ostia. Worse than that, this account is different from what Augustine said in his early letters. He had, for instance, a low opinion of Ambrose as a demagogic miracle monger in the days right after the man had baptized him. What has changed in *Confessions* is that Augustine now sees Ambrose as part of God's plan for him, and thanks God for the blessing.

If *Confessions* is not an autobiography, what is it (aside from its overall framework as a prayer)? It relives the drama of sin and salvation, in the form of a journey toward God. It stands closer to *Pilgrim's*

Progress, or even to *The Divine Comedy*, than to Rousseau's *Confessions*. It is a theological construct of a highly symbolic sort. An example of what might be called the autobiographical fallacy in dealing with *Confessions* concerns the famous scene in the baths of Tagaste. His father sees the sixteen-year-old Augustine naked and rejoices that he will soon have a grandson from this sexually mature youngster. Augustine says of that moment, "I was clothed in unstable (*inquieta*) manhood" (2.6). One psychiatrist, Dr. Charles Kligerman, takes *inquieta* to mean Augustine had an erection. Two other psychiatrists take it to mean he was masturbating.[1]

The masturbation fantasy shows a basic ignorance of the place of public baths in ancient life. They were very public, almost like our malls. Dinner guests met there for lavations before going to a man's house for dinner. Schoolboys were taught the decorum of the baths. Martial, the naughty Roman poet who revels in sexual scandal, finds little hanky-panky going on at the baths but towel-stealing. In Augustine's Africa, there were even hours set aside for nuns to attend the *thermae*.

The modern psychiatrists do not notice the truly odd thing about Augustine's phrase. If he is naked, why does he say he is "clothed" (*indutum*) in unstable manhood? He is thinking of a later "bath" in which he will go into the baptismal pool naked and come out clothed by Ambrose in a white garment, signifying that he is now "clothed in Christ." The text that hit him at the height of his crisis in the garden was Saint Paul's "Clothe yourself (*induite*) in Jesus Christ" (8.29, Rom. 13.14). This is also the first covert reference to Genesis, where Adam after his sin clothes himself in fig leaves, since he had lost the clothing of grace (*City of God* 14.17). Adam had become *inquietus*—Augustine's term for fallen mankind's heart, according to his famous statement at the opening of *Confessions*, usually translated "Our heart is restless (*inquietum*) until it rests (*requiescat*) in you" (1.1). Augustine's unquiet manhood is the sinful fallen manhood he inherited from Adam.

His father's look at his nakedness also has a parallel in Augustine's later "bath" with his spiritual father, Ambrose. The baptizand of that time had to undergo a physical inspection of the naked body (*scrutatio*) to see if any marks of diabolic affliction were present (*Sermon* 216.10). Every aspect of the baths scene is part of an antitype to the baptism that will reverse the effects of sin, which the worldly bath could not cleanse away. The psychiatrists who read the text as autobiography felt free to dig for deeper meanings of their own modern invention. The higher meanings that Augustine indicated by his language they missed entirely. We have to read Augustine as we do Dante, alert to rich layer upon layer of Scriptural and theological symbolism. We are not in the realm of autobiography but of spiritual psychodrama.

The Book's African Days

CHAPTER 3

Augustine begins his prayer with thanksgiving for his birth and for the care that was given him as an infant. Since he cannot remember his infant days, he conjectures what he was like from babies he has observed. The one he observed most closely, of course, was his own son, Adeodatus ("Godsend"). The boy was born of the woman Augustine lived with for fifteen years, in Carthage, Rome, and Milan. He was faithful to her all this time. As a Manichean, he prevented any further births by contraception, but he loved his son deeply and was proud of his precocity, cut off by an early death (at age nineteen). We can tell that Augustine is describing his son in *Confessions* because he uses the same description of a baby's language acquisition in the dialogue with Adeodatus at sixteen called *The Teacher*.

We should think of him, then, as looking at Adeodatus when he writes:

> You, God, who are my Lord, give life to the baby
> when you give it a body—we see how you articu-
> late its sensory apparatus, fit limb to limb giving
> beauty to its form, and coordinate all its instincts
> for self-preservation as a single thing. (1.12)

But since this prayer is also a theological profession of faith, Augustine finds signs of original sin
even in the willfulness of an infant:

> In time I began to smile, only in my sleep at first,
> and later when awake—so it was said of me, and
> I believed it, since we observe the same thing in
> other babies, though I do not remember it of my-
> self. Gradually I became aware of my surroundings
> and wished to express my demands to those who
> could comply with them; but I could not, since
> the demands were inside me, and outside were
> their fulfillers, who had no faculty for entering my
> mind. So I worked my limbs and voice, energeti-
> cally trying to signal out something like my de-
> mands, to the best of my little (and little availing)
> ability. Then, when I was frustrated—because
> I was not understood or was demanding some-
> thing harmful—I threw a tantrum because adults

did not obey a child, free people were not my slaves. So I inflicted on them my revenge of wailing. (1.8)

Then Augustine makes a claim that was hard to believe before Noam Chomsky published his studies of language acquisition. Augustine says he taught himself to speak by eagerly observing the connection adults made between certain sounds and certain things or acts. This resembles what three cognitive scientists have written in *The Scientist in the Crib*—that babies and toddlers experiment on adults in amazingly inventive ways.

After Augustine picked up the elements of one language (Latin), his knowledge and use of it would be refined by teaching in what we would call a prep school, for which he went away with his slave pedagogue to stay in another town, Madauros. When he could give his pedagogue the slip, he played hookey from school and went to games in the Arena (1.30). He also resisted those trying (with the help of resented floggings) to teach him Greek. His refusal to learn would later cut him off from the rich theological works of the Eastern Church. Why could he not learn Greek when he had taught himself Latin? He reflects that with Latin he observed words being used all the time around him to deal with immediate experiences, while Greek he had to learn solely from the page, which did not interest him.

> I applied myself to learning Latin words, without intimidation or coercion, surrounded as I was by nurses who coaxed, adults who laughed, and others fond of playing with a child. These words were learned without others' punitive insistence that I learn. From my own heart's need I went into labor to deliver my thoughts, which I could not have done without a stock of words, picked up not just from tutors but from anyone who spoke with me. Unfettered inquisitiveness, it is clear, teaches better than do intimidating assignments. (1.23)

He came back to his hometown of Tagaste when he was sixteen—this was when his father saw him in the baths. He was idle for a year while his father tried to raise funds to send him to what we might think of as college in Carthage. One night, with some fellow Tagaste teenagers, he stole a huge harvest of pears from their owner and fed them to another person's pigs. The emphasis on this peccadillo annoys some readers. They do not see why Augustine is eerily intrigued with his midnight naughtiness. Augustine is puzzled that the act was not done for any selfish motive, to eat or to sell the pears or give them to friends. It was an act of motiveless

pears

malignity—or so it seems to him at first. Why would boys demonstrate such utterly gratuitous malice as to destroy a man's property when no gain could come from it to the perpetrators? Almost any other sin is more understandable than this:

> Life in this world has its enticements because it accommodates us to its order, patterned to beautiful but lower things. . . . When the motive for a crime is sought, none is accepted unless the eagerness to get goods of the lower sort just mentioned, or avoid their loss, is considered a possibility. For they *are* beautiful, they *do* please, even if they must be abandoned for, or subordinated to, higher and more fulfilling goods. A murder is committed. Why? To get another man's wife or wealth, or to snatch at the necessities of life. Or for fear that someone would deprive the murderer of such things. Or from a sense of wrong burning for redress. Who murders with no motive but the mere murdering? Who would credit such a motive? (2.11)

Augustine admits that a favorite author of his, Sallust, accused Catiline of killing some people with no motive, making him gratuitously evil (*gratuito malus*). But Sallust contradicts himself in the same sentence, saying Catiline did have a motive—

to keep his criminal gang in practice (*Catiline* 16). That was clearly not the pear thieves' motive.

But by considering the sin more carefully Augustine does find a motive. He did it to keep in with his little gang, a thing he establishes for himself by reflecting that he would never have done it alone. He did it to be sociable, to enjoy a partnership (*consortium*) with the mischiefmakers. That word is a key one, since Adam was not fooled by the devil's blandishments—he ate the forbidden fruit to maintain his *consortium* with Eve (*City of God* 14.11)— an interpretation of the Fall that Augustine had enunciated in several of his commentaries on Genesis. Augustine knew Cicero's teaching that it is a perversion of friendship to stay with friends even ✓ when they are doing wrong (*Friendship* 42), and Augustine said that Adam's sin was a perversion of benevolence to a loved one.

> Adam yielded to Eve in breaking God's law, not because he believed she was telling the truth, but out of a compulsion to solidarity with her (*socialis necessitudo*), as male to female, only man to only woman, human to fellow human, man to wife. . . . He refused to be rent from this special partnership (*unicum consortium*), even at the cost of joining her in sin. (*City of God* 14.11)

Milton, in the most famous English account of the Fall, followed Augustine in making this the cause of Adam's action. He makes Adam say:

I with thee have fixed my lot,
Certain to undergo like doom—if death
Consort with thee, death is to me as life,
So forcible within my heart I feel
The bond of nature (*socialis necessitudo*) draw me
    to my own,
My own in thee. For what thou art is mine,
Our state cannot be severed. We are one,
One flesh, to lose thee were to lose myself.

Paradise Lost 9.952–59

One again, therefore, the text of *Confessions* is haunted by Genesis, by the story of the first sin. That was almost bound to be the case, given the elements of forbidden fruit, mysterious sin, and solidarity in the sin. Augustine gives us a further clue. Though he says that the thieves carted off "immense loads" (*onera ingentia*) of pears (2.9), he refers to only one pear tree—to make the parallel with Eve's fatal tree more obvious. Adam's sin was almost gratuitous—he did not do it for any gain—and it concerned an apparently trivial act, made serious only by the fact that it disobeyed God's easy command.

Augustine sees himself as re-enacting, in his own small way, the fall of humankind.

When he was seventeen, Augustine went to study in Carthage, the sinful big city. He had been taken under the patronage of the Tagaste millionaire, Romanian. Augustine either took with him from Tagaste or quickly found in Carthage the woman he would live with for the next fifteen years. Augustine again wanted to join a gang of troublemakers—they called themselves "Subversives" (*Eversores*)—who did things like burst into classrooms and disrupt them. He was too timid to join them in their more violent acts, but he wanted to be "one of the boys" swaggering about. "I associated with them but was ashamed not to match their shamelessness—since I kept clear of their raids, though I moved in their circle and had friends there" (3.6).

He joined a more serious forbidden set, the Manicheans, in Carthage. This was a Christian-Eastern movement that O'Donnell compares to New Age spirituality in our time. It said that spiritual light is trapped in material darkness, with Elect members struggling free of the body's toils and Hearers, held to lower standards, serving the Elect. Augustine became an enthusiastic and proselytizing Hearer. Like other Gnostic sects, the Manicheans rejected Jewish Scripture as primitive. But they were ardent followers of astrology. When Augustine's father died, his mother thought of moving in with him but was hesitant at first—not because of the woman he was living with (who soon gave her a grandson) but because he was a heretical Manichean. Her bishop in Tagaste told her that the fad would pass, and she joined her son in Carthage.

Though the Manichean religion was banned by the Christian Roman Empire, the practitioners were discreet and mutually supportive, not making a nuisance of themselves. Augustine found them a warm and welcoming body, and remembered with fondness his delight in their company:

> Some things about these friends entranced me—conversation and laughter and mutual deferrings; shared readings of sweetly phrased books, face-tiousness alternating with things serious; heated arguing (as if with oneself) to spice the general agreement with dissent; teaching and being taught by turns,; the sadness at anyone's absence, and the joy of return. Reciprocal love uses such semaphorings—a smile, a glance, a thousand winning acts—to fuse separate sparks into a single glow, no longer many souls but one. (4.13)

The ascetical ideals of the Elect seem to have prepared Augustine for deep reception at this time of

Cicero's lost dialogue, *Hortensius*. The aim of the work is to make a reader aspire to philosophy as a way of life. This set Augustine on fire, and raised the ideal of a fusion between asceticism and enlightenment (3.8). It was this time Augustine was remembering when he said that he prayed, "Lord, give me chastity and self-control, but not just yet" (8.17). Reading Cicero's dialogue made Augustine willing to look more closely at the Christian sacred writings, including Jewish Scripture, but the Manicheans had conditioned him to think them absurd, and their Latin translation in Africa offended his proud new rhetorical training (3.9). The rhetorical training was paying off for him in some ways. He won a poetry recitation prize given out by a prominent physician, Vindician, who would later become proconsul. Vindician led Augustine to question one aspect of his Manicheanism, a belief in astrology, against which Vindician made some scientific arguments that impressed Augustine, but which he still resisted (4.6).

After three years of higher rhetorical study in Carthage (370–373), Augustine went back to Tagaste, since Romanian, who was funding his study, wanted to give their hometown better educational opportunities. Once there, Augustine found an old school acquaintance whom he now made a close friend, persuading him to give up the Caecilian Christianity of his mother to become a fellow Manichean. But then the friend became deathly ill, and his family had him baptized (a thing often delayed until the point of death). To Augustine's horror, the friend decided, after recovery, to stay in the church from which he had received baptism. Augustine labored to argue and laugh him out of that resolve.

Shortly afterward, the friend did in fact die, and Augustine was plunged into a deep and angry depression. His pride was hurt that his own views had been rejected, and he resented what the friend took to be a blessing. He says, "I asked my heart why, in its anguish, it should violently whirl me about" (4.9). This echoes Psalm 41.5, "Why, heart, in your anguish are you whirling me about?" which in turn echoes God's rebuke to Cain when he resents Abel: "Why in your anguish are your features contorted?" The Latin Augustine used shows the parallels:

Interrogabam animam meam
quare tristis esset, et quare conturbaret me
    valde (4.9)

quare tristis es, anima mea, and *quare conturbas*
    me? (Psalm 41.5)

quare tristis es, et quare concidit facies tua?
    (Genesis 4.6)

When Cain objects to the favor God has shown to Abel, he is guilty of "sorrow for another's good fortune" (*tristia de alterius bonitate, City of God* 15.71). That is just what Augustine accuses himself of, when he resents his friend's happy reception of baptism: "He escaped my mad designs and found safety in you" (4.8). Reminded of his dead friend by his surroundings, Augustine abandoned the teaching Romanian wanted in Tagaste and "fled my homeland" (*fugi de patria*), going back to Carthage, the city of sin—just as Cain fled to a strange place and set up his own city, in Augustine's scheme of history founding the City of Man, as opposed to the City of God. Once again Augustine has found the patterns of Genesis when recalling in God's presence his own past life.

His mother Monnica returned with him to Carthage, and no doubt helped care for her grandson, Adeodatus. Augustine began to teach there, as he had in Tagaste. But he was looking for broader horizons, as he proved by writing his first book and sending it to Rome, hoping for praise from its dedicatee, the celebrity rhetorician Hierius (4.21). The book, now lost, was called *The Beautiful and the Decorous,* whose thesis he summed up this way (Letter 138.5):

> The beautiful, which we gaze on and praise for its own sake, has as its opposite the foul and ugly;

while the proper, whose opposite is the improper, is defined by what it is linked to, and cannot be assayed but in that connection.

Though Augustine had failed to argue his Tagaste friend back into the Manichean fold, he became a champion of that faith as the bright young schoolteacher of Carthage. As he would say in his book *The Manicheans' Two Souls*, "Arguing with ill-prepared Christians, I usually won a self-defeating victory (*noxia victoria*)." But under the glibness, he says, he was having doubts. When he voiced these to friends, they said he should wait till Africa's Manichean star, Faustus, arrived in Carthage. Augustine had been a Manichean for nine years at this point but had never met Faustus, and his expectations were high.

The hopes were disappointed when the two men met in 383. Augustine liked Faustus the man—handsome, charismatic, eloquent, an ascetic member of the Elect—but he got no real answers to his problems with the Manichean cosmology. "I did find him a gracious fellow, facile and talkative, repeating what they usually said but far more engagingly. Yet what help for my thirst was a deft waiter bearing a fancy chalice?" (5.10) Augustine brought up questions based on the liberal arts he was now teaching.

To his surprise, Faustus was not well versed in the common language of the learned in Late Antiquity. Disarmingly, Faustus was humble enough to admit this and to ask the younger man for some guidance. The person Augustine wanted to be his teacher now ∨ became his student. "I read with him any works he wanted to hear or that I thought appropriate to his stage of learning. But the better I knew him the less did I desire to go deeper into the teachings of his sect" (4.13) Augustine says he was now drawing away from the Manichean faith, though not from the social ties he had enjoyed throughout his two stays in Carthage: "I did not entirely renounce the religion, since I had found nothing better, and I was content to abide for a while where I chanced to find myself, until something better appeared" (4.13).

The odd thing is that the successful propagandizer of the Manichean faith found himself ineffectual with students in the classroom. The man who hated flogging and coercion in his own school days was not good at enforcing discipline. And, by a kind of poetic justice, the very *Eversores* he wanted to be part of now became a bane to his teaching. They invaded his classes:

> In Carthage, students disgracefully run wild.
> They feel free to crash into any class and with

> crazy grimacing destroy the order imposed for the students' benefit. With stunning obtuseness they inflict great damage, doing things punishable by law were they not accepted as common practice. (4.14)

Augustine was already pining to go to Rome, as we see from his sending his first book to a prominent orator there. Besides, he now heard that students in Rome were better behaved. He must have learned this from his main gossip vine, the Manicheans who were sheltering him. His patron Romanian was now one of them, and Augustine could not make an expensive move without him. He needed to take not only his wife and child with him, but scribes and slave attendants. To sneak this company out of Carthage, without letting his mother know what he was up to, took some careful planning; but he accomplished it, with obvious feelings of guilt. He sneakily deserted his native land, in a way that went far beyond his abandonment of Tagaste for Carthage.

The Book's Ambrose

CHAPTER 4

The sea voyage from Carthage to Rome was broken up by a stop in Sicily (the ancients were shore-huggers) and that meant only about a hundred nautical miles in open sea. But this was an agony to Augustine, one of the ancient world's worst sailors. He would only repeat the experience once, to get back to Africa four years later, resolved never again to set foot on the deck of a ship. He would praise his mother extravagantly when she faced such an ordeal in order to join him in Milan. Whether as a result of the journey or of his other ailments (Augustine was always ailing) or both, he began his first stay in Rome (383) deathly ill. He was nursed back to health by kindly Manichean contacts he had formed in Carthage. Augustine does not name a single one of these Manicheans who helped and promoted him for years—in this book as prayer, all that matters is his own blindness in embracing a heresy.

The pope in Rome when he arrived was the unsavory (but later canonized) Damasus I, at whose court Jerome was serving. But Augustine steered clear of the Christian community in Rome, for fear of exposing his Manichean fellows to danger. Those friends probably helped introduce him to those who preserved the surviving vestiges of paganism in Rome, another group at odds with the Christian Roman Empire. That conflict surfaced a year before Augustine arrived in Rome when some Roman senators, led by Quintus Aurelius Symmachus, protested the removal of the altar of the goddess Victory from the Senate House. The senators claimed that the goddess Victory had protected Rome for centuries, but the emperor Gratian, from his court in Milan, ordered her altar to be dismantled and removed. The senators formed a delegation to go to Milan and protest this decree, but Pope Damasus wrote ahead to the powerful bishop of Milan, Ambrose, to thwart the petitioners, and Gratian responded to this intervention by refusing even to see the delegation from the Senate.

There were many reasons for Augustine to get along with Symmachus, who was not only a famous stylist but a scholar (the editor of Livy) and a patron of scholars. He especially favored students of Virgil, and Augustine regularly taught rhetoric from Virgil's *Aeneid*. Augustine would also get his first impression of Bishop Ambrose, not a favorable one, from Symmachus. Ambrose had thwarted the first attempt to retain the altar, and Symmachus was preparing an elegant and detailed petition to restore the altar in the very year (383) Augustine arrived in Rome. Symmachus had some hope of success since Gratian, who ordered the altar removed, had been toppled by a coup. The leader of the coup drew up his army at the imperial court in Trier in Germany; but the Eastern emperor, Theodosius, supported Gratian's half-brother in Milan to be the Western emperor, though that man, Valentinian II, was only twelve years old. Symmachus addressed his petition to Valentinian, hoping he was weak enough at this point to be unable to resist his Roman subjects.

But once again Ambrose intervened. He had taken Valentinian's side against Maximus, and had favors to call in. But the boy-ruler's mother, Justina, was a foe of Ambrose. She was a patron of the Gothic part of the Roman army that supported Valentinian, and these soldiers favored Arian views on the Trinity that were anathema to Ambrose.

The bishop said that if Valentinian restored the altar of Victory, he would be refused communion in Ambrose's church. The petition was rejected in the summer of 384, just before Augustine left for Milan in the autumn of that year. He was going to the court of Valentinian as the imperial orator, a post traditionally filled from the more learned Roman part of the West, not from Milan itself. And it was Symmachus who, recognizing Augustine's rhetorical talent (despite his African accent), had recommended him for the appointment (5.23). Augustine was anxious to escape from Rome, where he had gone because the students there were more docile. But he found that they were also quicker to avoid paying their fees (5.22).

Augustine was carried by imperial carriage to the emperor's court just as a great struggle was beginning between Valentinian and Ambrose, one in which Augustine would try to remain neutral. This would be made difficult by his mother, who, learning of his great appointment, brought Augustine's brother, other relatives, and slave attendants to the court, hoping for material advancement—she would soon be arranging his marriage to an heiress. But his mother was pious as well as ambitious, and her Donatist-formed devotion to martyrs soon caused a problem with Ambrose. She wanted to continue the pious practices of her homeland (taking food to the martyrs' graves, fasting on Saturday). In *Confessions,* Augustine says that she gave up these devotions when she learned of Ambrose's opposition to them (6.3). But a later letter of Augustine tells a slightly different story. The newly arrived African woman asked her influential son at the court to request an exemption for her to keep her African ways. Augustine, no doubt embarrassed by the request, dutifully took it to the bishop and was turned down (Letters 36.32, 54.3). At that point, Monnica acquiesced, and she would soon become an ardent supporter of Ambrose against her son's employer, Valentinian.

If *Confessions* were an autobiography, we should expect an account of Augustine's work milieu, his duties and contacts in the imperial circle, his professional life. Instead, he just tells us he was paid to tell flattering lies to those in power (6.9, 9.13). He never describes the boy emperor or his imperious mother. The only time he names them is as persecutors of Ambrose (9.14). Instead, in his prayer, he thanks God for sending him to Milan to meet Ambrose: "You led me insensibly to him, that he might lead me sensibly to you" (5.23). He did not feel that way at the time. From Symmachus he would have been suspicious if not hostile to the man who had quashed his patron's petitions over the altar of Victory, and when he arrived in Milan Ambrose did not give him the time of day (6.3). Valentinian's lackeys were not the bishop's chosen company. When he describes himself as eager to consult the bishop, he says, wryly, "Ambrose is busy" (6.18). In *Confessions,* Augustine will no longer express the resentment he felt at the time. For that we have to turn to earlier writings. In *Dialogues With Myself* (Soliloquia 2.16) he says it was "cruel" of Ambrose to give him no guidance. And in an early letter to a friend after his baptism he says that they will not be the kind of philosophers who get enmeshed in worldly affairs—a clear hit at Ambrose (Letters 1.2).

Later, when Ambrose brought off a coup against Valentinian by producing martyr relics that worked miracles, Augustine thought this demagogic. Shortly after that event, Augustine mocked those "daunted by hollow claims of the miraculous" (*Order in the Universe* 2.2.7). Later, on the verge of his ordination as a priest, he wrote, "Miracles have not been allowed to stretch into our time, or the soul would always be looking for sensations, and the human race would grow jaded with their continual occurrence" (*True Religion* 46). Like most people in Late Antiquity, Augustine believed miracles were possible. But the devil was good at producing them, and Augustine thought there should be no attempt at competing on such ground. The Neoplatonic Augustine thought only philosophical argument should bring people to the truth. He would change his mind when he became a bishop himself, but, as James O'Donnell told me, "Augustine only begins to use Ambrose in later life when he needs him."

In this, Augustine stood apart from his mother, who entered gladly into Ambrose's great struggle around the celebration of Easter, 386. The imperial court had a basilica (the Portiana) outside Milan's walls where the emperor wanted to demonstrate his piety before the people on this great feast, and he had his purple tapestries hung there in preparation for his arrival at Easter. Ambrose knew that Arians would be admitted to the Portiana, and he treated the notice that this would be the emperor's service as a handing over (*traditio*) of church property to imperial/heretical use. He stirred up the people against this, and they tried to occupy the basilica ahead of time (after Palm Sunday). The rioters were arrested and fined, and an imperial guard was placed at the Portiana, to let people in but not out—let them starve there, if they wished. The stakes kept going up during Holy Week. The people in the Portiana sent a plea that Ambrose should join them. He sent some priests instead; but that act was used to say that he was fomenting disorder.

When it was learned that the purple hangings in honor of the emperor had been taken down at the Portiana and damaged, this was treated as an assault on the state. Ambrose refused to leave his own cathedral (the Basilica Vetus) except at night, for fear of being arrested as the instigator of these disturbances. (He had, after all, denounced the emperor's mother, Justina, as a Jezebel.) Loyal followers joined Ambrose in his church, where he led them in antiphonal choirs that laid the basis for Ambrosian chant (9.15). One of those singing most ecstatically was Monnica. "The community piously kept vigil in the church, ready to die with their bishop your servant; and my mother, who attended on you, was with the foremost in supporting him and keeping watch, her whole life turned over to prayer" (9.15)

Where was Augustine during this turbulent sequence? Standing aside, neither with his own fellow court officials nor with Ambrose. In *Confessions*, a decade after the event, he repents his not joining Ambrose. He says he was "more cool on the matter, since your Spirit had not yet thawed us" (9.15).

The court, intimidated by the popular support for Ambrose, removed the blockade of the Portiana on Holy Thursday, and repaid the fines exacted for the earlier uprising. What happened on Easter

Sunday is not entirely clear, but it is not treated as part of the struggle of that week. The court must have backed down in some significant way. Since the emperor shows up shortly after in Aquileia, he may have left for the church there on Friday or Saturday.

If Ambrose won this clash at Easter, the following summer he made a coup that brought him an overwhelming response from the Milanesi. Ambrose was about to consecrate a new basilica at the Garden of Philip in a western suburb of the city (the current Ambrosiana). This was a particularly sacred space for Christian Milan, since there were a number of martyrs' graves there (the ones, probably, that Monnica liked to frequent). Ambrose said that he had been prompted by the Holy Spirit to dig for new martyr relics there, to be installed in his new church. He turned up what he identified as the bodies of Gervasius and Protasius (whose names would become embedded in the Latin canon of the Mass). Confirming miracles were worked both at the unearthing and the installation of the saints' relics, and a pious delirium spread through the city. Monnica was no doubt part of this adulation, but we have seen already that Augustine disdained miracle mongering. In *Confessions*, he would change his tune, even saying that this was heaven's rebuke to his own boss, the emperor and his mother Justina (9.16).

By the end of this year in which he had looked with a cold eye on Ambrose's epic struggle with the boy emperor, Augustine would be ready to be baptized and join Monnica's church. What had happened in the interval? The traditional story, mainly based on *Confessions*, is that Ambrose's preaching had taught him how to read the Jewish Scriptures that had repelled him in his first encounter with them in Carthage. That, and the bishop's Neoplatonic approach to religion, won Augustine away from the Academic Skepticism he had adopted after abandoning Manicheanism. But a deeper look at what really happened is one of the many grounds people have had for attacking the historicity of *Confessions*. We have already seen, from other sources, that Ambrose had no time for Augustine. Instead, he went to two other sources of Neoplatonist teachings—Simplician and Mallius Theodore— who had more influence on his change of mind than Ambrose did at the time.

Simplician was a devout priest, but also the center of a Neoplatonist circle in Milan. He had been a close associate of Marius Victorinus, the translator of Plotinus, whom O'Donnell calls "the best Latin Platonist of the time" (3.6). Simplician was known for his lively relations with those who sought him out—he had been Ambrose's philosophical mentor, and he would be his successor as bishop of Milan. At a time when Ambrose was being "cruel" in dismissing Augustine, Simplician regularly received him (8.1–5, *City of God* 10.29). In later correspondence from Africa, Augustine would call Simplician "Father," and respond to enquiries from him with the words, "The heartfelt affection you show in your letter is not a new and untried vintage to me, but a familiar and treasured taste brought up from the cellars" (Letter 37.1). After leaving Milan, Augustine would never correspond with Ambrose, never dedicate a work to him, or request a book from him.

It is clear that Augustine had more immediate access to Neoplatonist thought in the person of Victorinus's friend than in Ambrose. And Simplician drew him into his philosophical circle, where Augustine met the man he most credited with his changed views at the time—though he is nowhere mentioned in *Confessions*. Mallius Theodore was a hero to Augustine because he had given up Roman office for a life of philosophy. He had risen from minor offices to become praetorian prefect of Gaul in 382. But he retired the next year to become a Christian Neoplatonist. Augustine had often talked to him about the true source of happiness, and on the eve of his baptism he dedicated to Theodore a book on the subject, *Happiness in This Life*. The dedication of that book shows how important Theodore was to him at this crucial point in his life:

Since, my Theodore, I look only to you for what I need, impressed by your possession of it, consider what type of man is presented to you, what state I believe I am in, what kind of help I am sure you can give me. . . . I came to recognize, in the conversations about God I held with our priest friend [Simplician] and you, that He is not to be considered as in any way corporeal. . . . After I read a few books of Plotinus, of whom you are a devotee, and tested them against the standard of the sacred writings, I was on fire. . . . So I beg you, by your own goodness, by your concern for others, by the linkages and interaction of our souls, to stretch out your hand to me—to love me, and believe you are loved in return and held dear. If I beg this, I may, helped by my own poor effort, reach the happiness in this life that I suspect you have already gained. That you may know what I am doing, how I am conducting my friends to shelter, and that you may see in this my very soul (for I have no other means to reveal it to you), I thought I should address you and should dedicate in your name this early discourse, which I consider more religious than my other ones, and therefore worthy of you. Its subject is appropriate, since together we pondered the subject of happiness in this life, and I held no gift of God could be greater than that. I am not abashed by your eloquence (why should that abash me which, without rivaling it, I honor?) nor by the loftiness of your position—however great it is, you discountenance it, knowing that only what one masters can turn a truly favorable countenance on one.

The later Augustine would mock the idea that true happiness could be found in this life. Though this was written after his so-called conversion in the garden and on the eve of his baptism, it shows that Augustine was, at this point, aspiring to a philosophical perfection rather than a Christian humility. After his baptism he would write to a friend that they must work to "deify" themselves. Just before his baptism, he wrote to another Neoplatonist friend:

I think we make enough concessions to our time if any pure stream of Plotinus is channeled through dark and thorny tangles to reach a few, rather than be loosed indiscriminately in the open, where its purity cannot be preserved from the random tramplings of cattle. (Letter 1.1)

After he had abandoned this rather snobbish attitude, he would have many reasons to regret his work dedicated to Theodore. In his *Reconsiderations* (1.2), a survey of his works at the end of his life, he wrote, "It is unfortunate that I gave more credit than he deserved to Mallius Theodore, to whom I dedicated the book, however learned and Christian he was." Another reason for his regret over Theodore is that the man he admired for abandoning a worldly career returned to it and rose to be consul. In *Confessions* itself, where he will not even name the man he once thought brought him to the truth, the unnamed Mallius is called "one puffed with outsized self-inflation" (7.13).

Well, if Augustine did not mainly get his Neoplatonism from Ambrose, what about his typological way of reading the Jewish Scriptures? That was a mainstay of Ambrose's sermons, and Augustine says he attended them—at first just to judge, as a professional, Ambrose's rhetorical prowess. On a superificial level he actually preferred his old Manichean guru, Faustus:

I brought a technical interest to Ambrose's discourses with the congregation, not for the motive

I should have had, but to see if he lived up to his reputation. Was he more or less eloquent than report had registered? Weighing carefully his style, I treated the content with a lofty disregard. I approved his easy fluency, which was more learned than that of Faustus, but—in style at least—less witty and charming. (5.23)

But as he listened, he says, what Ambrose was saying began to seep into him almost unconsciously:

Though I did not care to learn what he was preaching, only to hear how he was preaching it—this silly interest being all I was capable of, since I had no expectation that he could bring me to you—yet some of his content, which I was not following, slipped into my thoughts along with the style I was following closely. (5.24)

That passage confirms those who claim that Augustine learned his typological reading of the Scripture from Ambrose's sermons. But this seems unlikely. It does not fit well with the Neoplatonist readings that most occupied him in this time when he was consulting with Simplician and Mallius Theodore. Augustine was still detached from Ambrose in the summer of 386, and he left that autumn for a long time away from him. (Ambrose also off during that time, in Trier.) Augustine would not see the bishop again until the next January. He spent the next six months at a rich friend's villa, Cassiciacum, taking his mother, some friends, some pupils, and the attendant scribes and slaves, for a reorientation of his life.

From that safe distance he resigned his position at court, informed Ambrose that he wanted to be accepted for baptism in the run-up to Easter, and asked the bishop for suggested readings. Ambrose sent word that he should read Isaiah, but Augustine says he could make no sense of that prophet—an unlikely thing if he had learned Ambrose's typological way of interpreting the prophets from his sermons. Though Augustine wrote three dialogues in his retreat at Cassiciacum—a breakthrough after the long silence after his first (lost) book—none of them has any deep reflection on Scripture, typological or otherwise. They are pious, but in a philosophical way.

Admittedly, he would get an insight into Ambrose's typological technique when he submitted to the bishop for baptism. Ambrose treated baptism, to his catechumens, in terms of various foretypes in the Jewish Scripture. The bath of the soul was like the emergence from Noah's flood, or the passage through the Red Sea, or the water that

Moses struck from the rock, or the water that floated Elijah's axe (Ambrose, *Sacraments* 2.2, *Mysteries* 1.3). And the enactments of the ritual itself would bring home some of Ambrose's lessons. But in fact the use of Scriptural "types" would not be apparent in Augustine's writing after the baptism. It was not till four years later that they became prominent: when he was forced into the priesthood, he asked his bishop to give him some time to get ready by a deep study of Scripture. James O'Donnell says that this can be considered a deeper point of change in Augustine than the baptism itself. From this point on he would absorb a number of lessons from Ambrose that were not evident when he actually knew him. And when, six years after that, he wrote *Confessions*, he would thank God for the grace of taking him into the orbit of Ambrose.

The Book's "Conversion"

CHAPTER 5

The most famous passage in *Confessions* is the garden scene in Milan, from July 386, always referred to as the conversion scene—the moment when Augustine decided to be baptized. This is the second most celebrated conversion in Western Christian history, the first being Paul's on the road to Damascus. The only problem, in Augustine's case, is that it was not a conversion—not in the way that most people think of it. We usually talk of conversion as a change of religion—she was converted to Christianity, or Judaism, or Islam. But Augustine did not change his religion in the garden. He had already done that beforehand. The Neoplatonists of Milan had removed his last objections to Christianity— his inability to conceive of a totally immaterial god, or to go beyond Academic Skepticism. He tells us himself that "I no longer questioned the fact there is one reality that cannot decay, from which all other realities are derived. Now I want more to rest in you than to reason about you" (8.1) His intellectual quest was over. What remained to be done?

The garden scene is about giving up sex. Why did Augustine think he had to do that before he was baptized? You did not have to be celibate to be a Christian. You did not even have to give up sex to become a priest. That was becoming the ideal, but not a mandate in the fourth century. One of Augustine's esteemed correspondents, Bishop Memor of South Italy, was the son of a bishop and he had a son who became a bishop—Julian of Eclanum, a champion of Pelagius and a foe of Augustine. Members of this cultured Christian family bred a man who attacked Augustine for his "Manichean" hatred of the body. They could point out that Scripture limited bishops to just one wife (1 Tim. 3.2).

There is no doubt that Augustine had great suspicion of the body's weakness. But he shared this attitude with a far wider community than the Manicheans. The fourth century was the high period for asceticism that went beyond celibacy. Peter Brown's great book, *The Body and Society* (1988), describes a time when "the desert fathers" were international celebrities. Symeon Stylites, who famously fasted on top of a pillar, was consulted by the emperor Theodosius, and his advice was sought on church councils and political decisions. He had hordes of imitators. Heroic (and competitive) fasting repeatedly brought saints to the verge of death. Such people admired the scholarly Origen of a century before, who asked a doctor to castrate him so he could be freed of fleshly demands.

Many strands were interwoven in this extraordinary combat of the spirit with the body—Neoplatonic dualism of form and realization, Gnostic aspirations to a higher enlightenment, Stoic defiance of mere circumstance, and the belief that only self-control (*continentia*) could give one a manageable self. For some, the "mind-storm" of a sexual orgasm seemed an abandonment of Reason itself. This was a bias found at that time in the highest examples of the classical ideal. The emperor Marcus Aurelius gave up sexual intercourse as soon as his duty of providing an heir had been met. He called intercourse merely "an internal rubbing with spasmodic spurting of slime" (*Meditations* 6.13).

Augustine had connected philosophy with asceticism since the time he read Cicero's *Hortensius*— the book that made him pray God, even as a Manichean, to make him chaste (though not yet). He would have pursued this ideal even if he had never been baptized into the Christian community. In this he was typical of the intellectual aspirations of his time, not an exception to it. When discussing the matter with himself before baptism, in his *Dialogues with Myself* (*Soliloquia* 17), he does not make celibacy a religious duty, far less one connected with the priesthood (which he had no intention of joining), but a necessary initiation into philosophy:

> Portray woman as you will, endow her with every good thing, yet have I made up my mind that nothing is more to be shunned than union with woman. I know nothing that so topples a man from the defense of his own soul's battlements than female attractions and the carnal couplings that are the condition of having a wife. If a philosopher is allowed to beget children—a point I am not sure of—then he who has sex only for that purpose gets my admiration but not my imitation. The risk is greater than the chance of success. I have therefore laid this demand on myself (rightly and usefully, I believe)—to protect the freedom of my soul by giving up any concern or quest or contract with a wife.

When he assembled his close companions in Milan for a philosophical retreat, Verecundus, a rich teacher of literature, said he could not join them because he was married. "He said he could not be a Christian in the only [celibate] way he wanted to be" (9.4).

Monnica, busy in Milan, dearly wanted Augustine to be a Christian, but not (necessarily) a celibate. She lined up a wife for him, and persuaded him to send back to Africa the woman he had lived with faithfully for the last fifteen years. The mother of Adeodatus stood in the way of Augustine's worldly advancement—she was of a lower class, moneyless, and probably illiterate. Monnica must have provided the funds for her return to her native land. And Augustine's reaction?

> Since she was an obstacle to my marriage, the woman I lived with for so long was torn out of my side. My heart, to which she had been grafted was lacerated (*concisum*), wounded, shedding blood. (6.25)

This is the language he had used at the loss of his friend in Tagaste:

> I held in my soul as it struggled against being held in, lacerated (*concisum*) as it was, and blood-smeared. (4.12)

He might live without his favored woman, but he could not, yet, live without sex. In fact, he tells us he is not interested in marriage for anything but assuaging his sex drive (6.22). The heiress Monnica had provided for him was not yet of marriageable age (twelve), so he took a temporary mistress. He did not resort to promiscuity but to another sole lover—yet of course he bitterly rebuked himself for that (6.25). He was selling out his philosophical ideals, as Alypius reminded him (6.21). It is the struggle to break his addiction to sex that takes place in the garden.

Augustine contrasts himself with his boyhood friend, former student, and closest associate, Alypius, the lawyer who had come with him from Africa to Rome and then to Milan. Alypius had tried sex in his youth and been repelled by it (6.21). He wanted to make another try in Milan, just to see what Augustine was addicted to, but Augustine argued against this (6.22) Augustine congratulated him on his innocence. Since Alypius is going to be the witness to his garden experience, Ambrose decides to give a character sketch of the man. This is one of the two parts of *Confessions* that seems adapted from something written before. Paulinus of Nola had requested a mini-biography of Alypius, and Augustine probably wrote something to mark his friend's consecration as bishop of Tagaste in 394.

No part of *Confessions* fails more than this to maintain the atmosphere of a prayer. We learn of

Alypius's addiction to blood sports in the amphi-
theater and how he painfully overcame it (6.11–13).
We see him arrested on a false charge of theft, and
escaping by his reputation for integrity (6.14–15).
We hear of his judicial proceedings and his immu-
nity to bribes (6.16). He was too honest even to
have books copied for his private use at judicial
rates (6.16).

Just as Augustine was struggling between the
idea of marriage and of ascetical philosophy, he was
told—providentially, he believes—a series of tales
about men renouncing the world. These are commonly called "conversion stories," meant to foster
his own conversion, but that is true of only one of
the seven stories. The other six do not have to do
with adopting or changing religious views. They
are, more properly, vocation stories, tales of people
already Christian who are called to an act of renunciation. The first (renunciation story 1) was told to
Augustine by his Neoplatonist priest-friend and
mentor, Simplician, and it concerned the Neoplatonist author from Africa, Marius Victorinus, whom
Simplician knew.

Victorinus had come to accept Christian doctrine, but hesitated to be baptized for fear of losing
the esteem of his pagan admirers. He assured Simplician that he was already a Christian in his secret

life—to which Simplician answered that he would never really be a Christian till he was seen in a Christian church. Victorinus jested back, "Is it walls that make a Christian?" (8.4). But at length Victorinus made a very public profession of faith at his baptism. Simplician told Augustine this story because he saw an exact parallel between Victorinus's situation—a Neoplatonist balking at baptism—and Augustine's (8.10) But of course, it was not sex that was holding back Victorinus—it was worldly reputation. We do not know if Augustine confessed to Simplician his problem with sex.

Augustine takes this occasion to worry whether it is proper to boast of "celebrity conversions" like that of Victorinus. He concludes that it is, because Paul in Acts of the Apostles (13.7–12) boasts of converting Sergius Paul by changing his own name to Paul as a kind of victory claim (8.9). (Modern scholars do not accept this explanation of Paul's name.) The tale of Sergius Paul (renunciation story 2) is the only conversion from one religion to another in Augustine's account, and it is not, like the others, something told him in Milan. It is part of an argument he is making with himself about famous converts.

The next story involves four people, two men and two women—or, rather, five, since one story motivates the four. The tale of the four (renunciation stories 3, 4, 5, and 6) is told Augustine by Pontician, a fellow African at the court who drops by to visit Augustine and Alypius in their dwelling. When he sees Paul's letters in their room, he tells of two Christian fellows at the court who gave up their positions and their fiancees to become hermits—upon which their future brides pledged themselves to the same course of action. What inspired them all was chancing upon the life of Anthony the Hermit supposedly written by Athanasius (8.15). Augustine will add the details of Anthony's renunciation later (8.29) giving us renunciation story 7. Anthony heard in church the passage of Matthew's Gospel (19.21) in which Jesus tells his followers to sell all they have and give it to the poor. These stories show the power of narrative, whether read or spoken, to affect lives. They set up the story that Augustine will tell about himself in the garden. This whole sequence is shaped with great artistry. Now Augustine the dramatist takes over.

The way Augustine integrates these stories into his book shows great narrative skill. One of the courtiers Pontician is describing addresses the other courtier in his company. Since Pontician was not present at that scene, the speech Augustine gives the courtier is his own invention, and it echoes something that went before and prefigures what will come after. Here is the courtier's speech:

Please tell me what, with all our busy striving, we are trying to reach. Where are we going? What keeps us in [the imperial] service? Is it the highest post at court, as the emperor's intimates? But what distinction is more risky or unstable? How many perils will we have to face to reach a post of even greater peril? And how long must we labor to get there? Yet God's intimate I can become on the spot, merely by wanting to be. (8.15)

Augustine is clearly arguing himself away from the court he served. His prospects there were described earlier:

What a great thing is advancement to honorable office—who could ask for anything higher? It provides a circle of great patrons. If we give all our effort solely to this pursuit, a minor governorship at least should be attainable. Marriage to a woman of some wealth would be necessary, to provide expenses. This could be the extent of my ambition. (6.19)

The courtier's speech harks back to that passage, and looks forward to this:

I went to Alypius with storm on my face and in my mind, and burst out: What is the matter with us? Has it come to this? Did you hear that story? Non-philosophers surge ahead of us and snatch heaven, while we, with our cold learning—we, just look at us—are still mired in flesh and blood. Just because they have got ahead, should we be ashamed to follow at all, rather than be shamed at least into following? (8.19)

Prompted by Pontician's story, Augustine goes into a garden with Alypius. He feels he must make a decision, must break finally and forever with his sex addiction. But he feels unable, even at this late date. He describes his struggle vividly. But then, after such a drumbeat of renunciation stories clearly leading up to Augustine's own major act, the book brings in a retarding motion, building suspense. First, he puzzles over his ability to make his body react to his anguish, but not his will.

When tearing my hair, pounding my head, hugging tight my knee with laced fingers, I was doing exactly what I willed for my body—the willing would not have been followed by this effect if my limbs' response had been blocked. Yet I could not do what I far more eagerly wanted to do, and which I should have been able to do at will, since what I wanted to do at will was—to will. (8.20)

He concludes that the will is damaged by the heritage of sin descended from Adam, which leaves him with "a partial and wounded will, one jerking and lunging, part of it surging, part sinking" (8.19). He delays this self-analysis to argue that the divided will is not the same as the two wills posited by Manicheans, based on the two natures, one good, one bad, of their theology. He argues that there is a bewildering variety of desires tugging at the will. Often a person is most divided over choices that are all good or all bad. "If different wills make for different natures in man, there will not be two such but many" (8.23).

After this six-paragraph foray into theories of the will, Augustine returns to the great difficulty he experienced in willing the renunciation he wanted to will. He describes himself, with rhetorical alliteration, as "churning and chafing in my chains" (*volvens et versans me in vinculo me*, 8.25). His efforts all seem baffled, but he is edging toward the goal: He is "held more loosely now, but held." The strain is conveyed in vivid words:

> My inner self was urging me, Now is the time! Now! With those words I was moving toward a resolution, I was almost there—but was not there. Still, I did not slide all the way back, but braced

myself nearby, getting my wind back; then, renewing the effort I was almost there—almost—and just I touched, just grasped the prize. But, no, I was not there. I touched not, grasped not, not ready to let death die in me so life might live in me, my ingrained evil thwarting my untrained good. (8.25)

At this point he paints two symbolic scenes to dramatize the stakes in his fight against sexual addiction. In the first, his past sins swarm upon him:

My entrenched lusts, plucking me back by my fleshly clothing (*vestem meam carneam*), whispering low, Can you cast us off? And: From this moment, never more to be with us! And: From this moment, never more to do *this*, not ever, or to do *this*! What they specified by *this* and *this*, keep far from me, God—what sordid, what disgraceful things they spelled out for me. Yet I less than half adverted to their words, since they no longer flaunted themselves before me on my way, but were tittering behind me, as if furtively picking at me while I pulled away from them, trying to make me look back. And held back in some measure I was, not willing to break off, to reject them finally, to cast my self forward to what was calling me. And harsh old compulsion was all the while asking, Can you live without them? (8.26)

This imagined scene, with its repeated questions, is now balanced with a contrasting symbol, also asking questions:

Off in the direction I was turned toward, though I was afraid to advance into it, Lady Self-Control in all her chaste majesty (*casta dignitas Continentiae*) was revealed, serene, quietly mirthful, smiling me toward her, lest I hold back. To welcome and to hug me she reached her holy arms out, and in them were throngs of persons setting me their example, innocent boys and girls, young men and women—all ages, including chaste widows and women still virgin in old age. . . . She teased me with a smiling insistence: Can you not do what all of these have? Or do you think they did it by themselves, without God their Lord? He it was who gave me to them. Why do you stand alone, which is no standing at all? Throw yourself on him. Do you think he will not stay your fall? (8.27)

At last, after all these preliminaries in the garden, Augustine moves toward the climax. Though the last two sections have been clearly symbolic, not literal, what follows is taken by most readers as factual reporting—Augustine moves away from Alypius, throws himself under a tree, hears a voice telling him to read, takes up the letters of Paul, and reads, "Clothe yourselves in Jesus Christ." This is the moment recalled in many paintings. It is not surprising that Pierre Courcelle caused an earthquake in Augustinian studies when, in 1950, he claimed that the scene is just as symbolic, just as non-literal, as the two that precede it in the text.[1]

A first point for Courcelle is that Augustine, having put himself at some distance from Alypius, throws himself down "beneath a certain fig tree" (*sub quadam fici arbore*, 8.28). It seems odd to get horticulturally precise at this climax of spiritual drama. Courcelle rightly says the tree is there for its "symbolic force" (*valeur symbolique*, p. 193), and he connects it with the tree under which Nathaniel's thoughts are read by Jesus (John 1.47–48).

From under the tree, Augustine hears a child's voice from a nearby house (*de vicina domo*, 8.29). Courcelle thinks Augustine is presenting this as an angel's voice, since he says he cannot tell whether it is a boy's voice or a girl's voice. Courcelle thinks this is Augustine's way of saying it is *neither* a boy's voice or a girl's, since they are easily distinguished (a thought that might surprise all the boy sopranos in Bach cantatas). To strengthen his case, he relies on a single manuscript that reads not *de vicina domo* but *de divina domo* (from the divine house)—though

Augustine's normal way of referring to heaven is not as *divina domus* but *domus Dei* (God's house).

The voice chants repeatedly, "*Tolle! Lege!*" (Lift! Read!). Augustine goes over to an open copy of Paul's letter to the Romans and reads, "Give up indulgence and drunkenness, give up lust and obscenity, give up strife and rivalries, and clothe yourselves in Jesus Christ the Lord, leaving no further allowance for fleshly desire" (Romans 13.13–14). Courvelle takes the voice as a providential inner prompting which had guided Augustine to read Paul in this period—not just one text, but the whole teaching as it was gradually borne in upon him.

Courcelle begins to get into trouble in the next sentences, since Augustine goes back to Alypius, explains what had happened to him, and Alypius takes the codex out of his hand and reads the next words, "Welcome him whose belief is weak" (Rom. 14.1). This sets what is happening entirely apart from the imagined scenes of sins plucking at Augustine or Lady Self-Control gesturing toward him. No one "saw" those but Augustine—they were in his head. But the whole scene with Alypius has a witness, a very credible one, the lawyer-bishop of Tagaste, with whom Augustine was in constant communication in the period when he wrote *Confessions*. Is he making his friend complicit in a pious charade?

We know what he thought of such didactic pretending when Jerome, to save the reputations of Saint Peter and Saint Paul, said they only feigned a dispute at Antioch (the one described in Gal. 2.11–14). He wrote a whole treatise on deception to show that one cannot spread the truth with a lie.

The details of this section show that Augustine is not just talking in symbols. Alypius's change of heart is a real conversion, a change of religion, as opposed to Augustine's response to an ascetical vocation. Augustine had already been convinced, before he ever reached the garden, of the doctrines he took to be the essence of Christianity. Alypius was not. He had no issue with virginity, it was his natural bent. But he did not, till the moment in the garden, accept the truth of Christianity. His lawyer's mind was resisting. That is why he took Paul's words, "Welcome him whose belief is weak," as aimed at him personally.

James O'Donnell (3.60) scores strongly against Courcelle:

It would be easier to accept that the scene contains a heavy dose of consciously fictional elements (as opposed to a stylization of historical ones) if Courcelle had adduced other passages where Augustine makes up pretty little scenes out of whole cloth and passes them off as his own eye-witness testimony.

There are many things to indicate that the core story at this point is about real happenings. Augustine's uncertainty over the voice (boy's or girl's) is genuine. He tries to think of a child's game that would call for such a chant, and cannot (8.29). The Dutch scholar Alexander Sizoo has suggested that Augustine was genuinely puzzled, since he was hearing an Italian harvest chant he would not have known in Africa.[2] "Lege" regularly means "pick" or "select" as well as "read." If the chant was "Lift! Sort!" in the child's mind but "Lift! Read!" in Augustine's, then the very misunderstanding would guarantee the narrative's authenticity.

But, though the basic story is factual, that does not mean that Augustine did not see scriptural symbolism in the events. After all, he did that for most of the major parts of his story—the episode in the baths, the pear theft, the death of his friend. No major objection to the historicity of those stories was raised before Courcelle. The *meaning* of sheer event is searched for by Augustine in the light of God's action in the world, using his revelation as a key. So, in the garden scene, the fig tree was obviously there—it was a natural place for it. What bothered Courcelle was not its presence but why Augustine would mention it at this time. The answer, it seems obvious, is not to be sought in Nathaniel's tree—what has Nathaniel had to do with *Confessions* to this point? On the other hand, Adam's tree is very appropriate, and is part of the constant reference to Genesis.

The sin of Adam made him realize for the first time that he was naked, and he and Eve wove leaves from a fig tree to cover their shame. Remember that Augustine in the baths was "clothed in unstable manhood," as part of Adam's heritage in him, and he has just referred to his past sins plucking at "my fleshly clothing" (8.26). He will be clothed again in innocence as he comes from the baptismal pool, and that is what he thinks Paul is referring to in the Romans passage when he says, "Clothe yourselves in Jesus Christ."

But that does not exhaust the symbolic layers of meaning in this story, as in the whole book, the need to read theological layers upon layers as with Dante. One aspect of Augustine's agony in the garden is so obvious that it is surprising it has hardly been noticed. There is, after all, a most famous agony in a garden, that of Jesus at the Mount of Olives. Some have thought Augustine's description of his emotional anguish in the garden is overwrought

(8.29). But it is no match for the description of Jesus' suffering in the garden. He is sorrowful unto death, so worked upon that he sweats blood, so afflicted that he asks that the cup of suffering pass him by—though he finally accepts what the Father wills for him.

Augustine, too, is tortured unto death—"dying to be alive" (8.1). He is asked to undergo a suffering sent by God, who is "wielding a double whip" over him (8.25). Though he does not sweat blood, he is drenched "in great sheets of showering tears" (8.28). Lest we miss the obvious parallels, Augustine tells us that he withdrew from Alypius to undergo his agony alone, before rejoining his friend to go forth to baptism—as Jesus brought three friends into his garden, withdrew from them, then rejoined them to go forth to the crucifix. Augustine in this scene is going from the first Adam, clothed in sin, to the second Adam, whose redeeming death allows him to clothe himself in grace. Augustine re-enacted the fall of man in the pear scene. He now re-enacts the rescue of man by virtue of the suffering of Jesus, undergone for his sake. The most famous scene in *Confessions* is justly celebrated. It has depths below depths.

The Book's Baptismal Days

CHAPTER 6

Book 8 of *Confessions* ends on a misleadingly serene note. As Augustine finishes reading the passage from Paul, "light was flooding my heart with assurance, and all my shadowy reluctance evanesced" (8.29). He rushes to tell his mother that he will give up the wife she had planned for him, and she experiences "a chaster, sweeter joy than she had looked for from grandchildren born of me" (8.30). It seems that all struggle is over. This version of events has been useful to people who want "conversion" to be a sudden and final thing—men like William James (*The Varieties of Religious Experience*, chapters 9 and 10) or Arthur Darby Nock (*Conversion*). But modern psychological studies indicate that conversion—especially stable conversion—is far more often a gradual matter.[1] Not surprisingly, therefore, writings from the immediate aftermath of Augustine's garden experience give a less simple account of what happened with him than does *Confessions*.

In *Confessions*, the months spent in spiritual retreat at Cassiciacum are presented as all sunny friendship and ecstatic chanting of psalms. But what he actually wrote at the villa sounds several different notes. Augustine is holding on to his new resolve with a doggedness that says he would sacrifice friends to maintain it (*Soliloquia* 1.20). After boasting to himself that he had escaped sexual temptation, he admits that he was tortured the night before by "imagined caresses soliciting with the old bittersweetness" (*Soliloquia* 1.8). In his *Answer to Academic Skeptics* 2.2, he asks, "Who ever so suddenly felt such a thunder-stroke and a lightning-flash of self-control as to put a stop in one day to the ferociously deep-seated libidinessness of the day before?" Looking back ten years later, in *Confessions*, Augustine may have seen the garden experience as the point where the tide of battle turned, and he thanked God for the grace to escape his addiction. But it cannot have seemed so simple a matter at the time.

Augustine had spent three weeks after his garden experience finishing up his summer term of teaching. Then he went off to his friend's villa at Cassiciacum, from which he resigned his post at court, glad to give up the trade of phrase salesman (*venditor verborum*, 9.13). Augustine spent late autumn and early winter at Cassiciacum, and it was cold under the Alps. Alypius, to express his new penitential fervor, walked barefoot on the icy ground (9.14) Augustine, who had pled chest pains in resigning his rhetorician's office (9.4, 13), must have suffered from the weather. He says he experienced at the villa a toothache so severe that he could not talk—he had to communicate with the others by writing. But the prayers of the group relieved his pain, a sequence he describes as particularly wrenching: "What kind of pain could this be? And what kind of relief? I admit, my Lord and God, it frightened me. Nothing like this had happened to me in all my years. You were signaling to me in my depths" (9.12).

Augustine took great comfort in singing the psalms at Cassiciacum. He especially favored one, Psalm 4, in which the psalmist typically defies his enemies: "How long, human offspring, will your hearts be downward-thinking? Why love hollow things and seek the false?" He imagines singing this triumphantly to his old Manichean fellows:

> I wished they could somehow be near me, without my knowing they were there, to see my expression

as I sang Psalm Number Four in that place of con-
templation. They would have seen the effect on
me of its words. . . . They would have to overhear
me without my being aware of them, or they
would think I commented on the words with
them in mind. But in truth I would not have had
the words to say, or the right way of saying them,
if I knew they could hear and see me. And if I
could say the words, they would not have recognized them as my mind's inmost and most feeling
converse with and to myself about you. (9.8)

While he was at Cassiciacum, Augustine taught
his son and the son of his old and continuing patron, Romanian, lessons in Virgil. He also found
time to write his second, third, fourth, and fifth literary works—*Against Academic Skeptics*, *Happiness
in This Life*, *Order in the Universe*, and *Dialogues
With Myself*, 60,000 words in all—in the course of
three months (November–February, 386–387). All
of these were dialogues, taken down by shorthand
experts and immediately copied out over and over
again by scribes (he sent some back to friends in
Milan as they were finished). He does not mention
any of these by name in *Confessions*, but says only:

My books record the discussions held there with
the others and with myself in your presence. They

were written to serve you though they still panted
with a proud air, as if I were still puffing after a
run. . . . Alypius at first was fastidious about the use
of Christ's name in my dialogues. He wanted those
works to breathe the refined air of the schools,
more like high cedars the Lord stormed down than
the church's herbs for healing snakebite. (9.7)

Some think Alypius was still holding back from a
full commitment to Christianity; but that seems
unlikely after his garden experience and the fervor
he showed in walking barefoot on ice. He may have
been piously unwilling to introduce the sacred name
into what are largely classical secular dialogues mod-
eled on those of Cicero.

The dialogues themselves explain why Augustine
praises Monnica and Adeodatus in this part of
Confessions. Both impressed him by their intelligent
following of the discussions. Monnica especially
surprised him. Uneducated and perhaps illiterate
(O'Donnell 3.115), she was shrewd and funny in her
contributions to the dialogues.[2] He had no occasion to observe this of her before Cassiciacum,
where he says, "I am daily struck by your natural
ability."[3] When she says something that Cicero
had written, Augustine tells her, "You have taken
straightaway the high point of philosophy."[4] When

one party to a dialogue objects to Augustine's claim that the mind feeds on wisdom, she objects:

> Didn't you show us, just today, where the mind is fed from, and where? After eating a bit, you said you had no idea what was being served, since you were thinking of something or other. Where was your mind when you were eating without knowing it?[5]

Even Augustine's sexist comment about her is revealing for its day: "Forgetting her sex, we almost thought that some important man had joined us."[6]

Adeodatus, only fifteen, is ready to go to baptism with Augustine and Alypius. "We treated him as a peer in your favor as we underwent our education in your teachings" (9.14). Adeodatus will die at seventeen, outside the narrative timeline of *Confessions*, but Augustine takes this occasion to pay tribute to him:

> He was finely made by you, about fifteen, but already more intelligent than many older and more learned men. I testify to the talents you gave him, my Lord God, who make everything and can reform what we deform, since there was nothing of me in my son but my sin. You and none other inspired us to bring him up in your

teachings [i.e., his mother was a Christian while Augustine was a Manichean]. I testify to these your doings.

One of my books is called *The Teacher*, in which he speaks with me. You know that all the ideas he expresses in this dialogue with me were his own, though he had only reached the age of sixteen at the time. I had observed even more astonishing things in him. His talent was intimidating, and who but you could frame such a wonder? You took his life away early, but I am content, having nothing to fear from his conduct as a child or a youth or (if he had become one) a man. (9.14)

The narrative part of *Confessions* should reach its natural goal when Augustine is clothed in Christ by baptism. But he keeps the rule of secrecy around the rite itself (the *disciplina arcani*), telling us nothing about what happened when he, Adeodatus, and Alypius went naked into the baptismal pool and were clothed in white on the other side by Ambrose. He only tells us what his reaction was:

How many tears I wept at your hymns and canticles, abruptly carried away by the sweetly tuned voices of your church. The voices flowed in at my ears, your truth distilled in my heart, a wash of emotion arose in me and overflowed in tears, and they were a comfort to me. (9.14)

Here, logically, the story part of the book should end. The story's goal was always the baptismal font (now buried under the Piazza in front of Milan's cathedral, but excavated after World War II). But after the baptism, Augustine and his party leave for Africa, and Monnica dies at the port of Ostia ⌐ before they can embark. Augustine extends the logical shape of his story to bid her a farewell there.

This, like the brief life of Alypius, has the feel of something written beforehand—perhaps as a memorial to Monnica written for his sister, brother, and son (as the Alypius tribute may have been addressed to Paulinus). The formal note is struck when he says, "You give me warrant to speak for all [the company around her], Lord, since before her death we all lived as one community with her" (9.22). But since Monnica died after his story's end, Augustine included a tribute to his mother, just as he had shoehorned in a brief tribute to his son. His son would not die until Augustine and he had been back in Tagaste for a year, and it was hard to extend the story that far, suggesting a new chapter to be explored on native ground. But Augustine can take us down to Monnica's last days in Ostia. without too much strain:

The tribute is to a real person, not to what became the Western church's sacred figurine of "Saint Monica" (Roman spelling, not African). In the whole course of *Confessions*, Augustine has not been afraid to show Monnica's shortcomings, any more than he shied away from Alypius's addiction to blood sports. He says of her earlier days that she had not actually fled Babylon but was loafing (*tardier ibat*) on its outskirts (2.8). He criticizes her for not baptizing him in his childhood (1.18) and for not urging him to marry in his youth (2.8). In the social marriage she finally arranged, she shared Augustine's worldly ambitions, both for him and for others in her family.[7]

It would later be a common view that Augustine was dominated by his mother. The evidence is all against that. He was hardly an obedient son. He defied Monnica on the matter of sexual continence, saying he would have blushed at being so "womanish" as to heed her warnings (2.7). He remained a Manichean for a decade despite her laments over this and her initial reluctance to live under the same roof with a heretic. He lied to give her the slip when he left Carthage for Rome (5.13). He did not, for some time, share her enthusiasm for Ambrose—he was not with her in the bishop's church when it was threatened by the emperor (9.15). He did not share her credulity over the miracles around the relics of Gervasius and Protasius. It is extremely doubtful that he shared her belief that she could tell divine dreams by their odor (6.23).

Augustine writes about his mother as they waited in vain at Ostia (Rome's port city) for a ship to take them back to Africa. The usurping emperor Maximus had moved from Trier to Milan, and the Eastern emperor Theodosius was blockading the ports of Italy to keep Maximus's fleets inoperable. Augustine's party going to Tagaste was forced to stay in Ostia to wait for the next sailing season. Augustine took the opportunity to deepen the new estimation of his mother he had gained at Cassiciacum. She was about to die in Italy, though no one realized that for a time (9.23).

Monnica confided to her son a sin of her childhood:

Her parents, trusting her good behavior, used to send her down to fetch wine from the cask. She put a dipper into the opening at the top and, before she poured the wine into a jug, she would take a little taste, just touching the tip of her tongue to it. She did not drink more because she did not like the taste. It was not a need for drink that motivated her but the extra energies of youth, which overflow in playful antics, customarily repressed in young spirits by their elders From one taste she gradually added more, sip by sip—since to neglect things is gradually to slide down—until she had fallen into the habit of draining the cup when it was almost full. (9.18)

Augustine and Monnica thank God that he sent a corrective to this vice:

A slave girl, who used to go with her young mistress to get the wine, had some quarrel with her. When they were by themselves, she used the harshest insult to accuse her, calling her "a wino" (*meribibula*). This stabbed home. Recognizing her own foul conduct, she instantly condemned and repudiated it. As flattering friends mislead, quarreling foes can often correct. (9.18)

Monnica became a model wife, as that was understood at the time:

Her actions spoke of you, and you made those acts so beautiful that her husband respected this admirable, this amiable wife. She put up with his marital infidelities, never quarreling over them, expecting him to become chaste when he became a believer by your mercy toward him. She also knew that, for all his great goodwill, he had a fiery temper, and opposing an angry husband, by deed or even by words, does no good. She waited, rather, for the moment when his storm had passed and he was calm, then quietly made her own case, as if he had just acted out of unconsidered irritation. (919)

As a result of her restraint, her husband Patrick (this is the only time his name is given in *Confessions*) never beat her, and she became the counselor and consoler to wives who were beaten (9.19). She was the general peacemaker of her community in Tagaste (9.21).

Augustine was away from his hometown for most of the time when she was so important to it. First he was at "prep school" in Madauros for three years in his early teens (366–369), then at "college" in Carthage for three years (370–373), then for six years at Carthage as a teacher (376–383). He had little knowledge of home life with his family at Tagaste. No doubt he heard much from his sister and his brother. But the main assessment of his mother's role there probably came in her reminiscences during her last days in Ostia, when he at last became close to her. Of that time he remembers: "We talked in the sweetest intimacy" (9.23). One moment was particularly important. The two were standing at a window, looking out on a garden—like the garden in Milan in his moment of renunciation, but this one more the Garden of Eden than the Garden of Olives, since they talked of what the blessed life in eternity could be. Their speculations together he puts in a single tour-de-force sentence, as they asked each other things like this:

> If fleshly importuning were to fall silent, silent all things of earth, sea, air, silent the celestial poles, silent the soul, moving (oblivious of self) beyond the self; silent, as well, all dreams and internal visions, all words and other signs, silent everything that passes away, all those things that say, if one listens, We did not make ourselves; He made us who never passes away; if after saying this, they too were silent, leaving us alert to hear the One who made them, if He should speak, no longer through them but by Himself, for us to hear His word, not as that is relayed by human tongue or angel's voice, not in cloudy thunder or dim reflection, but if we hearken to Him we love in other things without those other things (as even now we strain upward and, in a mind's blink, touch the ageless wisdom that outlasts all things), and if this

were to continue, all lesser vision falling away before it, so that this alone held the universe in its
grip, in its enfoldment and its glad hidden depths,
and eternal life resembled this moment of wisdom
that we sigh to be losing—would that not be what
is meant by the words, "Enter the joy of your
God?"—a joy that will be ours, when?—only
when "all rise though not all are changed"? (0.25)

In this sentence, the step-by-step shooshing of the
universe mounts by anaphora (silent . . . silent). The
glimpse of "ageless wisdom" comes in a fleeting way,
as a grammatical aside. Then, after this quiet climax,
the sentence falls off, fragmenting as the vision is
dispersed, ending (in a dazed way) with questions.

Brilliant as that sentence is, it cannot be literally
how the conversation went between Monnica and
her son. Augustine admits that it is a distillation of
what they were talking about, presented to her afterward as a kind of summary: "Something like that
is how I described our experience to her, not in just
that tone or those exact words" (9/26). Once again,
as so often in *Confessions*, the problem of historicity
rears itself. It is clear why Augustine would remember, ten years later, one of his last conversations
with Monnica as so revealing. But it makes no sense
for that time. What Augustine is describing is an

ascent, up through created ranks of temporal being, to the eternal Creator. This was an ascent he had tried as he became a follower of the Neoplatonists (7.23), but he was baffled in the attempt, he recalls, because he was still too mired in time and materiality. He thought then that a course in the liberal arts would free the mind to soar toward the eternal.

What was surprising, even shocking, about his near-success with his mother is that she was not a learned Neoplatonist freed by the ethereal exercises of the liberal arts—or that is the lesson he later draws from his memory. But we know from the Cassiciacum dialogues, written within a year of his stay with her in Ostia, that he still had the belief that bliss could be reached by mental ascent, even here—that is the whole point of his dialogue *Happiness in This Life*, and his claim that Mallius Theodore had reached the happy state. Later he will see that only life with God, after death, can give such happiness, and Monnica's resignation stands for that truth:

> You, Lord, know what she responded after our conversation on that day, in which the world and all its joys came to seem, in the process of our talk, utterly worthless—she said: As for myself, this world holds no more delight.

In his revised view of the mental ascent to God, Augustine would no longer try to reach an eternal ecstasy in this life. He would see the highest attempt with Monnica as a hint, a touch, of the joy that can only be given by heaven. In *Confessions*, he gets that insight through his mother; and in the next book he gives a Christian version of the longing for God held out here below, but only as a foretaste:

> What, in loving you, do I find lovable? Not, surely, physical splendor, nor time's orderliness—not light's clarity (how kindly its aptness to the eye), nor sweet linkages of variable melody; not soft fragrances of flowers, oil, or spice; not honey or heaven-bread; not limbs that intermingle in embrace—these are not what, in loving you, I love. And yet I do—*do* love a kind of light, a kind of song or fragrance, food or embrace—in loving you, who are my light and voice and fragrance and food and embrace, all of them deep within me, where is my soul's light that fades not, its song that ends not, a fragrance not dispersed in air, a taste never blunted with satiety, an embrace not ending in depletion. This is what, in loving my God, I love—yet what can I call this?
>
> I interrogated the earth, which replied, I am not it—and all earth's contents gave the same

testimony. I interrogated the sea, its depths with their slithery inhabitants, which informed me: We are not your God, go higher. I interrogated the veering winds, and the entire atmosphere, with its winged breed, replied to me: Anaximines was wrong, I am no God. I interrogated the cosmos— sun, moon, stars—which said: No more are we that God you are in quest of. So I addressed the entirety of things thronging at the portal of my senses: Tell me then of the God you are not, tell me something at least. And, clamorous together, they came back: He is what made us. My interrogation was nothing but my yearning, and their response was nothing but their beauty. (10.8)

In his prayer long after the event, Augustine finds in his last conversation with his mother the key to his later insights into a faith that supplanted his philosophy of his early days after baptism—as he later saw what he considered the significance of Ambrose in his life. Neither thing was obvious at the time. But in thanking God for his guidance away from the past, he is right to see more than he was taking in at the time.

It is poignant that Augustine was beginning to see qualities that he had ignored in his mother just before she died. After describing their conversation by the garden, he writes, "Little more than five days after this, she was struck with a fever. One day in the course of her illness, she fell into a coma and was no longer aware of her surroundings." She came out of the coma long enough to talk with her sons Augustine and Navigius and her grandson Adeodatus. Navigius is not named in *Confessions*, but he had come with his mother and other relatives to see what prospects there were for the family in Milan, and he had been a named participant in the dialogues at Cassiciacum. In Ostia Monnica told her sons, "Bury your mother here."

> I, fighting back my tears, did not answer, but my brother said something to the effect that he held to the brighter prospect of her dying at home, and not abroad. At the words she winced and directed a reproachful glance at him for such thoughts. Looking at me, she said, "See what he can still be saying." A little later she said, "Bury me where you will, don't let it bother you. One thing only I ask, that wherever you are, you remember me at the Lord's altar." After expressing this wish, so far as her weakness let her, she fell silent, in agony as her illness worsened. (9.27)

During her feverish days, but before the coma, she talked with friends who were surprised that she did not want to be buried where family and friends could tend her tomb (she had, remember, been devout in visiting the martyrs' graves in Tagaste). She answered, "Nothing is far from God—I have no fear that, when the time comes, he will not find where I am, to raise me up" (9.28). Augustine adds, "In the ninth day of her illness and the fifty-sixth year of her life, when I was thirty-three, her devout and observant soul was separated from her body."

Augustine cried immediately when Monnica died, but checked himself when he saw his son effusively weeping for his grandmother. He and the others told Adeodatus that this was not the Christian way:

> We all agreed that it would be wrong to celebrate her funeral with tearful complaining of lament. These are the customary indications that one has died in a bad state, or else entirely ceased to be. But she was in no such condition. (9.29)

This whole section is meant to contrast with the wild and Cain-like wailings Augustine had indulged at the death of his friend in Book 4. Accordingly, Monnica's funeral was celebrated with joyful psalms, and Augustine was very contained at the funeral (9.30). Later, trying to sleep, he remembered one of Ambrose's poems (9.32):

> To knit up tired limbs,
> Rebuilding them with rest,
> Restrengthening our minds,
> With anxious cares oppressed.

After waking from that sleep, he could shed gentle tears of remembrance (9.33). The detailed, almost day-by-day tracing of his psychological reaction to his mother's death lends support to the hypothesis that this part of the story was written at the time of that death.

The Book's Hinge

Book 10 steps away from what Augustine has written about himself up to ten years ago, and asks two things. First, why did he tell his own story in the first place, as part of his prayer of repentance for sin and thanksgiving for grace? He could have prayed in silence, and not in writing that other people could read. He told us in Book 8 how narratives of Christian progress and renunciation helped him. He hopes that others will find the same benefit in overhearing his prayer: "The virtuous are interested in the tales of sinners who have repented, not because the sins interest them but because, though they once occurred, they do so no longer" (10.4).

But now that he has broken off the story of his past sins, why is he continuing his prayer in writing? He answers: "Many have asked about my condition at this moment of my testifying—both those who have known me and those who have not, but have heard something from me or about me" (10.4) We saw in chapter 1 how this passage has been used to claim that Books 10 through 13 were added later to Books 1 through 9, and we found how little sense that makes. But the puzzle remains. Why take his readers with him through an clabo- ← rate examination of conscience at this point? The reason is that he wants his readers to go through the preparation for reading the deepest mysteries of Genesis. This is an act of ritual cleansing.

Augustine tells us that even as bishop he is beset by temptations. He accuses himself of certain lapses, but these seem petty and the thorough search for them is strained, especially since he uses a scriptural checklist to cover all bases. Some people, including James O'Donnell, think this is the most boring part of the book. But they miss the point. There is a quality of ritual here, not surprisingly. It is part of a long religious tradition to make a confession of sin when approaching the altar—or, in this case, the holy writings. Western cathedrals usually had scenes of the Last Judgment carved outside or painted inside the entry portal. This was to prompt a repentance of sin before coming near the holy place inside. At the beginning of the Mass, priest and people confess their unworthiness in the Confiteor. The priest repeats the prayer of prophets that their tongue and lips be cleansed as by fire. Augustine, as he is about to open his treatment of Genesis, prays: "Circumcise my lips from every rash or deceptive utterance, outside or within me. Purify my delight in your Scriptures so I am not misled in them myself nor mislead others" (11.3). Augustine's self-examination is not a form of self-indulgence. He is like an athlete warming up, getting his body ready for a challenge.

But why, it may be asked, does he begin this elaborate self-scrutiny with a long excursus on the subject of memory? A superficial answer is that he has to consult memory to find out if he has been tempted or lapsed from virtue. But a deeper answer is called for by the thoroughness of the section on memory. More than any other writer—more than Bergson, even, or Proust—memory is the key to Augustine's thinking because he thought it the key to his own identity. He knows who he is only because memory connects events in his life over time. Without memory he is a series of disjunct happenings—like an amnesiac he has no name, no connections with other human beings, and no clues to the existence and action of God. Memory creates the self, which is why—when he seeks analogues to the Trinity in himself (made in God's image)—God the Father, the creator, is like memory:

> In memory's immense courtyard are sky and earth and sea made present to me, and whatever I sensed in them (except those I have forgotten). And this is where I bump up against myself (*mihi et ipse occurro*) and call back what I did, and where, and when, and how I felt when I was doing it. (10.14)

One thinks by sifting memories, finding patterns. One can recall sin without sinning again, or "predict" the future from memory's recurrences (at dawn the sun will rise because I remember it always doing so). Yet memory, the very stuff of oneself, is mysterious to oneself:

> I go out onto the lawns and spacious structures of memory, where treasure is stored, all the representations conveyed there by any of my senses, along with the further expressions we derive from those representations by expanding, contracting, or otherwise manipulating them; everything ticketed (*commendatum*) and stored for preservation (everything that has not been erased in the interval, everything not buried in oblivion). Some things, summoned, are instantly delivered up, though others require a longer search, to be drawn

from recesses less penetrable. And all the while, jumbled memories throng out (*proruunt*) or, while something else is being sought, flirt out (*prosiliunt*) to block the way, as if teasing: "Wasn't it us you were seeking?" My heart's hand strenuously waves these things away from my memory's gaze, until the dim thing sought arrives at last, fresh from depths. Yet other things are brought up easily, in proper sequence from beginning to end, and laid back in the same order, recallable at will—which happens whenever I recite a literary passage by heart. (10.112)

Memory is a kind of inner exploration, a probing of many potentialities:

Vast, my God, is the power of memory, more than vast its depths, immense and beyond sounding— who could plumb them to their bottom? Even though this is a power of my own mind (it is what I *am*), still I cannot take it all in. The mind is too limited to contain itself—yet where could the uncontained part of it be? Outside itself, and not in itself? Then how is it itself? Over and over I wonder at this, dumbfounded by it. Men go out to wonder at mountain heights, at immense sea surges, the sweep of wide rivers, the ocean's range, the stars' revolvings—and neglect the spectacle of themselves. (10.15)

The memory can even remember that it has forgotten something—which seems an act of self-destruction. How can this be?

> Here I labor at hard material, Lord, and I am that material. I am "a terrain of trouble" [like Adam's], worked with much "sweat of my brow." What we are doing here is not, after all, studying heaven's distances, not measuring interstellar spaces, not poising earth on balance. I am what I am remembering, my own mind. It is no surprise for some non-me to be distanced from me, but what is nearer to me than I myself? I cannot understand myself when I am remembering, yet I cannot say anything about myself without remembering myself. And what am I to make of the fact that I am positive that I remember having forgotten? Shall I say that what I remember is not in my memory? Or that forgetting is in my memory, to remind me to forget? Both are the purest nonsense. (10.15)

Augustine comes to a tentative solution for this problem. Since memory is dynamic in Augustine, a constantly shifting and kinetic phenomenon, the forgotten thing is experienced like a lost limb throwing off the customary motion. When it experiences forgetting, it is "as if the memory had some feeling that it was not moving with something it had moved with before, but was limping, as it were, from the lack of what it was used to, and trying to recover what was missing" (10.28). The defective motion indicates a certain loss.

Augustine puzzles out the mysteries of memory at such length because it is the only way he has to know himself. He is constantly performing experiments upon himself:

> The scope of memory is vast, my God, in some way scary, with its depths, its endless adaptabilities— yet what are they but my own mind, my self? Then what can that self be, my God? What is my makeup? A divided one, shifting, fierce in scale. In memory alone there are uncountable expanses, hollows, caverns uncountably filled with uncountable things of all types—some of them representations, like those of sensible objects, some present without need for representation, like the tenets of the liberal arts; while others are there by some mysterious registration process, like the mind's reactions, which the memory retains though the mind is no longer experiencing those reactions— still, if in the memory, how not in the mind? I rummage through all these things, darting this way and that, plunging down as far as I can go, and reaching no bottom. (10.26)

This recalls the Gerard Manley Hopkins poem, "No Worst":

> O the mind, mind has mountains; cliffs of fall
> Frightful, sheer, no-man-fathomed. Hold them
>   cheap
> May who ne'er hung there.

Since memory contains all Augustine has seen or known or thought out, he strives for another Platonic ascent above himself, but finds again that he cannot reach God in this life:

> I will pass beyond the scope of what is called my memory—for even birds and beasts have memory (or how could they find again their nests or lairs, or whatever other places they haunt, which could only become their haunts because remembered by them?). So I will pass beyond my memory in quest of him who sundered me from quadrupeds and made me wiser than the flighty birds. I will pass beyond memory to find you—where? Where, my sure and loving stay, shall I find you? If I find you beyond memory, is that not to forget you—would I be finding by forgetting you? (10.118)

He finds God only by a sense of what is missing, as he remembers forgetting. God is the constant absence in his making, according to the psychological

statics he had form͡ i early in *Confessions*: "You
made us tilr. rd you, and our heart is unstable
until stabilized ͬ you" (1.1). He seeks God in himself, as a mystery reaching toward mystery: "Our
mind cannot be understood, even by itself, because
it is made in God's image" (Sermon 396.2).

After the profound preliminary section on memory, the examination of conscience by Augustine has
a perfunctory air. He is checking off items on a list,
some relevant to his situation, some not. Most such
exercises have a mechanical air, like that of pilots
running through the items on a pre-flight survey of
the equipment, or like a doctor's rundown of physical possibilities in a patient's checkup. Actually, Augustine is less mechanical than might have been expected. Others have used the Ten Commandments
or the Seven Deadly Sins or the Seven Cardinal Virtues as their guides to spiritual danger. Augustine
uses a short formula from the First Letter of John
(2.16) to cover all the temptations that can face a
human being. In the Latin of his Bible, the Letter
said: "The things of this world are the urges of the
flesh, the urges of the eyes, and worldly designs."

Augustine likes to think in threes, and he was especially drawn to this passage while writing *Confessions*. As usual, he finds layers of meaning in the
threefold division. He sees it in the three tempta-

tions of Jesus in the desert. Satan asks him to change a stone to bread (urges of the flesh), to save himself from a fall by magic (urges of the eyes), and to assume a kingdom (worldly designs). He even finds in the temptations a perversion of the values of the Trinity—the Holy Spirit of love perverted by the urges of the flesh, the guidance of the Son perverted by magic urges of the eyes, the majesty of the Father perverted by worldly designs.

Given this grid for psychological self-examination, Augustine asks himself how, if at all, he has responded to the three temptations.

1. *The urges of the flesh* (10.39–53). This covers the sensual demands of the body—for food, drink, sex, comfort, repose, and so on. Augustine runs through the five senses to see how each responds to the urges of the flesh. Under the sense of touch, he asks whether he has any complicity in the sexual dreams that cause a nocturnal emission. If he were perfect, this would not happen, but he distinguishes imperfection from guilt:

> There are representations of things formed by preceding habit that linger in the very memory I have been delineating—representations that throng on me, though weakly, while I am awake, but with enjoyment in my dreams, where I yield to the

imagined act. So strong in my flesh is this fictive representation that sleeping falsehood prevails where waking truth could not. Am I not my real self then, Lord? Is there some border between two different selves which I cross and re-cross in sleeping and waking? What happens in this process to the self-rule that stays strong against such promptings, unbending under buffetings, even in the presence of real women? Does it go to sleep because the body's external senses do? In that case, how could we stay strong at times even in sleep, remembering wakeful resolve to stay chaste, not yielding to these sensual solicitings? Yet the border between the two selves remains clear enough that, when we do fail in dreams, we can awake to a clear conscience. Because of the distinction between the two states, we did not do willingly what we regret was done passively in us. (10.41)

He prays to be freed, eventually, from this imperfection.

The second sense he treats is taste, where he admits that he sometimes eats or drinks more than the body strictly needs:

I cannot resolve to abstain from food once for all, never indulging in it again, as I gave up sexual intercourse. The bridle on my appetite for food must be adjusted with calibrated tightenings or looosenings of the rein, and who, my Lord, can maintain the exact dgree of required tension? (10.47)

He prays for better adjustments of control over his appetite.

The third sense is smell, and he finds no desire for perfumes or sweet odors in himself. The fourth sense is hearing, and he rebukes himself for sometimes savoring hymns for their beauty apart from their devotional meaning. The fifth sense is sight, and Augustine has an aesthete's delight in daylight colors and an abhorrence of the dark:

> My every waking moment, sights brush across my eyes, not intermitted as sounds are when the cantor falls silent, or the choir does. For light, the empress of all colors, floods all things visible everywhere—wherever I am in the day, wooing me with its variable coloring even when I, at my tasks, am not adverting to it. But so powerfully pervasive is this light that our impulse is to call it back if it is suddenly removed, and to be depressed if it is gone for long. (10.51)

He prays to take delight in sights only as signs of God's creating goodness.

2. *The urges of the eyes* (10.54–59). Since he has covered the sensual delight of the eye already, he takes "urges of the eyes" to refer to a desire to see illicit things—that is, as an urge toward transgressive knowledge (*curiositas*). This covers magic, superstition, false prophecy, astrology—all things that have no appeal to Augustine since he gave up his Manichean interest in astrology.

3. *Worldly designs* (10.59–64). This is the temptation Augustine feels most threatened by. His position as bishop brings him prominence, and he enjoys that.

> I wish I were not elated by praise for good behavior—but elated I am by the tribute to good behavior, and just as dejected, I must admit, by denigration of it. And when this failing nags at me, excuses suggest themselves, how validly only you can tell, since I cannot be objective. (10. 61)

Virtue must be praised, for the edification of others. But Augustine is afraid of being praised for the wrong thing, or of growing too fond of the praise without acknowledging his need for God's grace. There is, too, a haughtiness in not caring for other people's opinion:

> Some people are vain of nothing but their own approval, whether others approve of them or no, not

even trying to win their approval. But you profoundly disapprove of self-approvers—they count as a distinction what disfavors them; or count real distinctions as their own, not as coming from you; or count them as coming from you, but by their own desert; or count them as your gift, yet not as something to be enjoyed with others, but to be withheld from them. You observe how my heart trembles at all three prospects, and all similar perils and toils. And I realize that I have not so much stopped wounding myself as that you have not stopped healing me over again. (10.64)

Now that Augustine has limbered up, doing his spiritual calisthenics, he is ready, with the help of grace, to plunge into the depths of mystery, to open the book of Genesis and find God there.

The Book's Culmination

CHAPTER 8

Though some readers drop out of the book when Augustine's life story seems to end, he tells us that this is the part he has been waiting for, and he cannot continue to hold back from the study of Scripture, which is his real goal:

> Even if I have the opportunity, still, to continue my narrative, the water drops of time are too precious for me to do so—I have for too long been burning with a need to study your law, to testify about what it is I understand and what I have no sense of— through the dawning of your light and the lingering shades of my own night—and how far my frailty has been taken up into your strength. I would not have any hours diverted from this, apart from those I must spend on the restoration of the

body, the drawing together of the mind's resources, and the service I owe, or pay without owing, to others. . . . Lengthen my days for the study of your law's inner meanings. Open the door to them when I knock on it. You had a purpose in causing the Scripture to contain so many pages dark with obscure meaning. This dense wood shelters deer who have taken refuge in it, restoring their strength, pacing its lanes and grazing there, resting and ruminating. Lord, make me complete for the receiving of these matters. Grant what I love, for the fact that I love was itself your grant. Leave me not, keep what you planted from withering. (11.2–3)

Augustine knows that understanding Scripture is difficult—that is what repelled him when he first looked into the Jewish Bible in Carthage. It is often said that he had learned by now how to read Scripture as allegory. That is not quite right. Nor does he use the mediaeval "fourfold sense" of Scripture. He is much more flexible than that, treating any passage according to what seems to him its concrete purpose in its place. He says, for instance, that God cannot have created the world in six days, as Genesis seems to say. The Bible cannot contradict what reason tells us, and reason, guided by Greek astronomy, tells us: that the earth is round. When it is day on one side, it is night on the other—so there is no such thing as an absolute Day One followed by an absolute Night One:

> If I said such a thing, I dread being a laughing-stock among those who are scientifically informed, who know that when it is night with us, the sun is shining on that part of the globe where the sun that set on us is traveling to rise again, since all through the twenty-four hours of its circling the earth there is day somewhere while there is night elsewhere. Surely we do not want to locate God at some point where night descends on him while day dawns at a different point![1]

God does not endorse the kind of literalism that Fundamentalists do. He is speaking symbolically, and his "first meanings" are what the symbols are trying to tell us.[2] Thus Augustine treats the opening of Genesis in three separate books of *Confessions* since he finds intimations of the Trinity in the overture to all Scripture.

God the Father: Creation (Book 11)

He begins with "At the origin God made the heaven and the earth." He contrasts this making with any kind of making we know—that of the craftsman, for instance, or the artist:

> You did not work like a human artist reshaping physical materials to give them the form seen within by the artist's directing mind. . . . You are the creator of the artist's body, of the soul that works its limbs, of the material he reshapes, of the talent that masters his art and devises internally what he will fashion externally, of the body's perceptual system that transmits his design from the mind into the stuff he works, and then reports back to the mind what was made, so it can compare it with the model to see if it corresponds with it. (11.7)

That kind of making occurs in sequence, and there is no sequence in God. When he "says" let there be light, his word does not sound in a material medium. It does not begin to resonate and end. There is no before or after. Though he creates time, it is from his own timeless eternity. How can that be?

To puzzle this out, Augustine begins by asking what is time—a question less obvious, he says, than we normally assume:

> If nothing were passing away, there would be no past time; and if nothing were still coming, there

would be no future time; and if nothing were passing, there would be no present time. But what mode of existence can those first two times have, since the past is no longer and the future is not yet? And the third time, the present, if it were not passing away, would not be the present but the eternal. But if the present is only a time because it is passing away, how can we say that it exists, since the reason of its existing *as time* is that it will soon not be, which means we only say it exists because it is on its way to non-existence? (11.17)

What is the presentness of the present? A "present minute" is actually the seconds that have passed and the seconds that are about to. Can any second as it flies by be fixed, or reduced to a point that is actually *there*, or does even the smallest second have a beginning and end and intermediate parts?

If we suppose some particle of time which could not be divided into a smaller particle, that alone deserves to be called the present. Yet it flies in so headlong a way out of the future and into the past that no bit of it can be fixed in pause. If it paused, its earlier part could be divided from its later. And if it stopped, it would no longer be time but eternity. (11.29)

Some say time—day and night, months and years—is what we know from the motion of the planets. But that is just a measure of time, as any motion can be. It has to have a medium through which things move and a way of charting the motion. None of these constitute time itself (11.30). Augustine finds no way to tell what time is from the things whose motion is being measured, but from the instrument that is doing the measuring—the human mind. If the present slips dizzyingly into the past, it slips into memory, which measures the experience of passing events by comparison with other such experiences. Once again, memory is the key to Augustine's thought. In a very early work, *Music* (6.21), he had argued that a word, or even a syllable, cannot be understood except by memory, since by the time the last part of the word is sounded or read, the early part—the clue to the whole—is in the memory.

Even the future is only an extrapolation of the expected from similar events stored in the memory. Thus there are not three tenses—past, present, and future—but three presents, the remembered present of a past experience, the present experience passing into memory, and the present future conjectured from the present memory of the past (11.26).

So time is produced by "the mind's two-way reach" (*animi dis-tentio*, 11.31):

> Say I am about to recite a psalm I am familiar with. Before I start, my anticipation reaches out (*tenditur*) to include the [remembered] psalm in its entirety; but as I recite it, my memory reaches out (*tenditur*) to carry into the past each thing I shall be cropping from the future, so my soul's life-force (*vita hujus actionis meae*) reaches in opposite directions (*dis-tenditur*)—into memory by what I have just said, into anticipation for what I am about to say—while simultaneously reaching out (with *ad-tentio*) to the present, through which what was future is being shuttled into what is past. (11.38)

Memory conducts the whole process, because my self—which is my memory—is enacting it.

Time thus depends on a kind of timelessness if it is to be understood at all. By memory I string together disparate episodes in time that show a continuity of myself outside the passing moment. I can recall sin without sinning, by an escape from past experience. I can connect with that past sin by remembering, in an escape from my present experience. I can resolve not to repeat the sin in the future, by an escape from anticipated events. Thus the excursus on memory in Book 10 was not a detour from Augustine's path but the preparation for the quest for God outside of time in Book 11. Augustine can partly grasp the idea of a timeless God acting in time by the way a human's time-bound mind strives up toward timelessness. But this striving is baffled precisely by time, a truth he did not grasp when he was hoping for a Neoplatonist ascent to happiness in this life:

Since your pity superintends men's various lives, behold how my life-force reaches in opposite directions (*ecce distentio est vita mea*). Your right hand has upheld me in my Lord, the son of man, who mediates between your unity and our multiplicity (for we are multitudinous in the multitude of things). Through him may I lay hold on him who has laid hold on me, and be gathered out of my useless years by following the One, oblivious of the past, not caring for the future things that pass away but for things prior to all. No longer reaching in opposite directions (*distentus*) but reaching forward (*intentus*) only—not with divided reach (*distentionem*) but with forward reach (*intentionem*)—I seek the prize of your high calling, where I may hear the song of praise and contemplate your delight, a thing not of the future or the past. But for now my years are passing amid sobs, with only you to solace them, Lord, my everlasting Father. I, however have been disarticulated into time (*ego in tempora disilui*), I cannot put time together in my mind, my very thoughts are shredded, my soul inwardly unstrung—till I flow together into you, purified, to melt into the fires of your love. (11.39)

God the Son: The Origin (Book 12)

Augustine is awed by the difficulty of reading Scripture. God is too far above his creatures for their language to express his nature. Speaking of Moses as the author of Genesis, Augustine writes, "He was addressing a crude and earthbound people, to whom he felt he could convey nothing but the visible works of God" (12.24)—not the invisible and timeless meanings he was trying to convey. Thus Augustine is patient with naive readings of the Scripture which mature readers must reject when they grow more sophisticated. The childish reader may think that God created the world as an artist creates in time, or that he sounded words in time to accomplish this—which at least gives them the core idea that everything comes from God.

> In these people, who are still little children nursed with simple formulas like infants in their mothers' arms, a useful faith is instilled, enough for them to learn and accept that God made all the wonderfully varied things they see around them. But if one of them spurns this simple language of faith, and flings itself in high pride from the nest that protects it, so that it falls, poor thing—God keep the little fledgling from being crushed by the feet of passersby. Then send your angel to take it back up to the nest, to stay there till it can fly. (12.37)

But such simple formulas are not proof against *heretical* misinterpretations, once such limited readings are strained by their application to God. Then a deeper investigation is called for: "For others, the biblical words are not a nest but a dense thicket. Glimpsing berries hidden there, they flit inside, merrily chirping as they spy the berries and peck at them" (12.38). Thus Augustine means to delve into the divine mysteries that are cloaked in human language. In the very first verse of the Bible, he sees that "At the Origin (*in Principio*) God made heaven and earth" cannot literally mean *at the beginning of time*, since

God's creative act is outside time. So *Principium* means the origin of form, God's Wisdom, his Son, the second person of the Trinity, through whom he acts to give being to all the things he makes. And "heaven and earth" are not the visible things we see but their principles, the primal spirit and unformed matter that are the principles of creation. These are later given lower expression as sky and earth, but their first conception is outside time, as sound is a precondition of the song that shapes it (12.40).

"Heaven" in verse 1 of Genesis is thus pure spirit, the "heaven's heaven" of Psalm 115.16 and "heavens' heaven" of Psalm 148.4. Heaven's heaven is form without matter, and "earth" is matter without form. They resemble Aristotle's argument that change only becomes possible by a combination of potency with act. "Prime matter" is an almost-nothing. Its activation explains the limits of created being as outside God's timeless act, which has no potency for change. Augustine is venturing onto new ground for himself, concepts he will soon be elaborating in his great book, *First Meanings in Genesis*. Here the idea of "heaven's heaven" as the highest form of created spirit is left obscure. It seems *personal*, since it *contemplates* God, but is sometimes described as if it were an impersonal principle. In the later book, he will more clearly specify angelic intelligences as "heaven's heaven." But even in *Confessions* he says, "*Let there be light, and there was light* is best taken, I think, of the creation of spirit, for it has a kind of existence capable of illumination" (13.4).

> As always looking on God face to face, and experiencing his Word, his only-begotten Son, equal to the Father, the holy angels are the first to possess created wisdom, and therefore to understand the whole of that creation of which they were the first realization, all of it comprehended in the Word of God, who contains the eternal patterns (*aeternae rationes*) of everything created through him, even those things that come about in time. Only after seeing first of all in his unchanging truth the patterns from which everything is made, do they glance below at what was actually made and return praise to him for what was done.[3]

Since God's actions are not sequential because outside time, everything he creates is created all-at-once, by a kind of spiritual "big bang." Time will unfold things implicit in this single act of creation. The first act contained primordial patterns (*rationes seminales*) for everything that will appear in its appointed time.[4]

> One might say, if you will, that when we read "At the origin God made heaven and earth,"

the heaven and earth referred to are not their completed and final reality, whether visible or invisible, but an inchoate and formless stuff shapeable and separable into distinct forms, with existing potentialities not yet apparent in their forms and qualities, but destined to be sorted out into their appropriate identities—heaven, namely, and earth, the spiritual and the material. (12. 26)

What will follow in sequence and be understood by time-bound humans is symbolically represented as separate acts, in language tempered to human imperfection. The first intelligences to grasp this are the angels, who see the primordial patterns partly as simultaneous, partly as sequential, in accord with their recognition of God's action on a level of being below his. Thus the "first day" is the light on the angelic intelligences, as these articulate the patterns of creation, and the following "night" is the angelic grasp of the created things that come from the *causae seminales*.[5] Augustine's concept of "Let there be light" as the enlightening of the highest intelligences is given visual expression in the cupola mosaics of the narthex to the basilica of San Marco in Venice. For the first day in that series of images, one angel contemplates what God is doing, for the second, two angels—and so on.[6]

Augustine recognizes the speculative nature of his reading of Genesis. It is the best he can do to reach the first meaning of the text, but he does not exclude other readings if they retain the essential truths—God's timelessness and the createdness of time.

God the Holy Spirit: The Protector (Book 13)

Since Book 12 was devoted to the Origin, the Wisdom in which all patterns are formed, it is no surprise that Book 13 will study the third person of the divine Trinity.

> I already recognized the Father in the words "God made," and the Son in the phrase "at the Origin," and since I believe in a triune God, I sought my belief in your holy pronouncements, and there it was—"the Spirit hovered over the waters." This passage contains the Trinity—Father, Son and Holy Spirit—the maker of everything made. (13.6)

Augustine's attempt to understand the mystery of the Trinity begins from his attempt to understand the mystery of himself. Since humans are made in God's image, the place to look for God is in the human soul or psyche or self. We are each a manifold yet united thing. Speaking of memory, Augustine had expressed amazement that people go all around the world looking for marvels but neglect their internal landscape and geography, more stunning than any external spectacle. God, he holds, can only be found through introspection. "The light was within me, but I was outside myself" (*Intus enim erat, ego autem foris*) (7.11).

> You were waiting within me while I went outside me (*intus eras et ego foris*) looking for you there, misshaping myself as I flung myself on the shapely things you made (*formosa quae fecisti deformis inruebam*). (10.38)

God, Augustine came to realize, is "deeper in me than I am in me" (*interior intimo meo*, 3.11). That is why he went spelunking after God. "Each person has himself at hand to study, to observe and ponder and report what he finds" (13.12).

In *Confessions,* then, he explores one analogy to God in the human makeup:

> A wise course were to reflect each on our own inner threefoldness—not that this is the same thing as the Trinity; but even the extent of difference, I would suggest, is worth examining, testing, and experiencing. For I find these three acts in us,

existing, knowing and willing—I do exist and do know and do will. My existence is a knowing and a willing one, and my knowledge is of a knowing and willing self, and my willing is for existing and knowing. Let anyone who is capable explore how inseparable in life are the separate existence, separate mind, and separate being, a separateness inseparable but still separate. (13. 12)

Later, in his long book *The Trinity*, he would refine and more deeply explore the analogies to the Trinity in himself, and memory (not existence) would then stand for the Father:

These three things—memory, understanding, and will—are not three lives but one life, not three minds but one mind, and therefore not three substances but one substance.

Memory, for instance, when it is called life or mind or substance, is being identified as separate to itself. But when it is called remembering, there is reference to something beyond itself (that is remembered).

The same holds true of understanding and willing. When called by those names there is reference to something beyond them (to be understood or willed). But each of them is, in itself, a life or mind or substance.

So all three are one, insofar as they share one life, one mind, one substance; and whenever they are named as such, the singular, not the plural, is to be used of each of them, and of all together. But they are plural, three, when each refers beyond itself to the others.

And each is equal to the others, taken singly or together, since each contains the others, either singly or together. In fact, not only does each contain the others, but each contains the totality of all three.

For I remember that I have memory, understanding, and will.

I understand that I have understanding and memory and will.

I will that I will and remember and understand.

And I remember all of my memory and understanding and will, all at the same time. If there is any memory I do not remember, it is not in my memory; for nothing can be more remembered than what is in the memory.

Thus my memory is of my *entire* memory.

Similarly, I know that I understand all that is in my understanding, and know that I will all that is in my will—and this knowledge, too, I remember.

I remember, then, the entirety of what I understand and what I will, and when I understand all three together, it is their entirety I understand. For when I do not know things that can be understood, they are not in my understanding. And what is outside my understanding I can neither remember nor will, since if I remember to will something understandable, it must be in my understanding.

My will in the same way contains the entirety of what I understand and what I remember, whenever I want to activate anything from my store of understanding or memory.

Since any of the three contains any of the other two, or all of them, they must be equal to any of the others, or to all of them, each to all and all to each—yet these three are one life, one mind, one substance.[7]

Augustine cautions that this multiplicity-and-oneness is only a thin shadow of the divine persons' triunity, but the mystery of man does open some dim path toward seeing the mystery of God.

The Holy Spirit is a bond of love between the three persons and between man and God. As the Spirit hovers above the waters, he draws men up toward him:

In the Spirit's gift we find our stability, there we enjoy you yourself. Our stabilization is our peace, so love tumbles us toward it, your Spirit's favoring will drawing our lowliness up from the portals of death. In that favoring will is our peace. A physical object tends by its specific gravity to find its natural level. It does not tend necessarily downward, but toward whatever its natural level is. Fire tends up as a stone tends down. Their specific gravity keeps them in motion till they find their own level. Oil poured out under water comes to the surface. Water poured out over oil sinks below it. Their specific gravity keeps them in motion till they find their level. Out of the proper place, they are unstable. In their proper place, they are stabilized. The specific gravity that moves me is love. By your gift we are kindled and borne upward, we are set afire, and we go, we ascend the heart's ascents and sing the climbing song. (13.10)

Augustine describes the action of the Spirit on three levels—in the single act of creation, in his forming love of the individual soul, and in his guidance of the church. Thus, "Let there be light" applies to the spiritual light in heaven's heaven, to the enlightenment of the believer's faith, and to the teaching of the church. And the creation of the "firmament," the canopy between upper and lower waters refers to the physical cosmos, to the scriptural guidance of the believer, and to the church as a shield. The equation of the canopy with Scripture comes from Augustine's use of Isaiah 34.4, "heaven will be rolled up like a scroll," and Psalm 93.6, "heaven is stretched out like parchment" (13.16). Scripture shields the mind protectively. The waters above the canopy refer to the fountain of life in the heaven's heaven (13.18).

In the same way, the creation of fish in waters refers to the "briney" creatures of Psalm 65.7 (13.20), who need to be saved by the waters of baptism (13.26), and the dry land is where safety and nutrition take place (13.29). The lights in the heavens are the saints that set standards (13.23). Augustine sees these polysemous messages reaching him through the holy words, without claiming only one interpretation as the proper one:

> Can I fairly be charged with misleading, with mixing categories, with failing to distinguish the radiant expression of truths in heaven's canopy from material creatures in the wavering sea or elsewhere under the canopy of heaven? The meanings of the former are fixed and defined, and do not increase from one generation to the next, but have the clarity of wisdom and knowledge. Yet their exemplifications in the latter, in the physical world, are

multiple and changing, as things increase and multiply by your blessing. You have ministered to the sluggishness of our mortal senses by letting one meaning have, in the mind's expression, varied symbolic representations in the activity of your material creation. The waters engendered such activity, but only as your Word intended. Such signs are engendered to suit the mental limits of those still distant from your eternal truth, but only as they serve your revelation. The need for these watery engenderings was human resistance, but what produced them was your Word. (13.27)

In this final book, then, the Spirit's love radiates downward through every level of the cosmos and the human mind and the soul. The vision is of a unity of divine action through every aspect of the universe, like that of Dante in the *Paradiso*, which appropriately quotes Augustine:

E 'n la sua volontade è nostra pace
    (*Paradiso* 3.85)
In bona voluntate pax nobis est (13.10)

The Book's Afterlife

CHAPTER 9

Early Reception, Later Neglect

Augustine tells us that *Confessions* was the book most frequently and favorably read during his lifetime. But not all notices of it were favorable. At the end of his life he drew up a list of his published works, to certify the authentic ones and make some comments on them. This work, called *Reconsiderations* (*Retractationes*) says, of *Confessions*:

> This work in thirteen books, testifying both to my bad and my good actions, praises God as just and beneficent, and directs human thought and emotion toward him. It had this effect on me as I wrote, and still does as I read. What others feel about it, let them find on their own, though I know that it has pleased many of my fellows, and still does. Books One through Ten are written

about me, and the last three about the holy Scripture, from the words "At the origin God made heaven and earth" through to the Sabbath repose. (2.6.1)

The reference to what others think sounds defensive, and it should, since there were early criticisms of the book. One early reaction would dog Augustine till the end of his life. He was told by a bishop friend that Pelagius, the ascetic theologian, responded violently when he heard a sentence from *Confessions* read out in Rome. Pelagius took it as a denial of human free will, turning humans into God's robots. One of Augustine's descriptions of what he heard about this event is from his late work, *The Gift of Continuing Fidelity* (20.53):

Which of my books has been read more and with greater approval than *Confessions*, which I issued before the Pelagian heresy arose? It is true that I said in it of God—and said frequently [four times]—"Require anything, so long as you grant what you require." When these words were read to Pelagius, by a friend of mine (and my fellow bishop) who was staying with him, Pelagius could not contain himself. Attacking the sentence with some passion, he all but treated his visitor as his adversary. Yet what does God first and foremost require but that we should believe in him? And this belief is what he himself grants when it is proper to say, "so long as you grant what you require." In that book, which told the story of my return—of God's returning me to the very faith that I had trashed with my sad and mad babblings—you recall, do you not, that I told how I was won by the faithful and daily tears of my mother, praying that I should not perish? I thus made the point that God by his favor can turn back men's wills not only when they are twisted away from the true faith but when they are turned to an attack on that faith.

Followers of Pelagius would keep up the attack on Augustine—Caelestius, and (especially) Julian of Eclanum, the bishop-son of a bishop-father, who engaged in a long mud-wrestle with Augustine. Though most of this had to do with other writings of Augustine, concentrating on original sin and free will and grace, Julian did take one side-swipe at a passage in *Confessions*, that where Augustine told of his mother's childhood drinking. Julian claimed that Augustine took a low view of marriage, and opined that he might have formed it from his parents' marriage: "You may indeed know of some secret taint in the marriage of your mother, since you brand her with the term 'wino' in your book called *Confessions*." Augustine fired back: "It is no wonder you come out as her foe, since you are a foe of the grace by which, as I wrote, she was freed of that childhood vice" (*Unfinished Answer to Julian* 1.68).

After these early skirmishes, attention to *Confessions* somewhat died down. Augustine was powerfully influential in the Middle Ages, but mainly for his doctrinal works (on sin and grace) or his ecclesiology (much of it misreadings of *The City of God* on the role of the church in society). There would be new attention focused on Augustine during the Protestant Reformation, since Reformers found him a useful alternative to the scholasticism of Thomas Aquinas, but here too *Confessions* was not the main work considered. Luther was more interested in Augustine's views on the doctrine of justification, and Calvin in his views on predestination, than on Augustine's personal story.

In the Renaissance, Erasmus (1469?–1519), who was briefly a monk in the Augustinian order, did a new edition of the works of Augustine, but he—like John Colet in England (1467–1519)—concentrated first on the book *Teaching Christian Faith* as a basis for a believer's humanism. Otherwise Erasmus mined Augustine's scriptural commentaries for his own editions of the Bible. Typically, the one part of *Confessions* that called for his special attention was the exegesis of Psalm 4 at *Confessions* 9.8–11. Just as typically, Erasmus came to admire Jerome far more than the less biblically learned Augustine. Some (but not Erasmus) in the Renaissance were Ciceronian purists, who objected to Augustine's flashy Latin style. That was an attitude still prevalent in the Enlightenment, as when Gibbon wrote: "His style, though sometimes animated by the eloquence of passion, is usually clouded by false and affected rhetoric."[1]

The "Great Sinner" Myth

Confessions re-emerged into floodlit attention in the Romantic era of the late eighteenth and early nineteenth century, when it was read as a *Bildungsroman* riding on the popularity of Jean-Jacques Rousseau's *Confessions* (1782) and Johann Wolfgang von Goethe's *Sorrows of Werther* (1774) and *Wilhelm Meister's Apprenticeship* (1795). In 1888 Harnack would compare *Confessions* to Goethe's *Faust*. The coming-of-age tale and sins-of-my-youth story made Augustine a byword for libertine-rake glamorization. Such is the reputation of *Confessions* that James O'Donnell said he first took up the book as a boy with the expectation that it had salacious things in it (for which, he added, he is still futilely searching). The "great sinner" myth has no basis in fact. As we have seen, Augustine had no time for promiscuity, since he took up instantly, at age seventeen or eighteen, with his common-law wife "and lived with this one woman and kept faith with her bed" for fifteen years, all through what is supposed to be his inflammable youth (4.2). When she was sent off as he prepared for marriage, he took up briefly—for just a matter of months, or even weeks—with an interim mistress. Those are the only two women he seems to have slept with.

This is hardly the stuff of great-sinner drama, yet Augustine is popularly known as a young sex hound. His own words play to this conception, since like all saints (even virginal ones, like Therese of Lisieux) he stresses the great distance of his own lowliness from God's purity. Even those who grant that he was not a promiscuous offender say that he was obsessed with sex. The record does not support this, either. Peter Brown points out that he does not dwell on sexual sins in his hundreds of sermons and letters, or such massive works as *The Trinity* or *The City of God*. "In a standard edition [of *The City of God*], out of sixteen lines devoted to deliberate human sins, only two refer to sexuality."[2]

He struggled to achieve celibacy, as did Jerome and other saints of his time; but he did not, as many people assume, think that sex was a matter of guilt in the unfallen state of Adam. The long argument on sex arose from his late struggle with Julian, who denied the effects of original sin. Augustine said that loss of control over one's bodily responses was one effect of Adam's fall—not only the problem of unwanted sexual temptation but of unwanted failure to perform sexually.

> At times, without intention, the body stirs on its own, insistent. At other times, it leaves a straining lover in the lurch, and while desire sizzles in the imagination, it is frozen in the flesh; so that, strange to say, even when procreation is not at issue, just self-indulgence, desire cannot even rally to desire's help—the force that normally wrestles against nature's control is pitted against itself, and an aroused imagination gets no reciprocal arousal from the flesh.[3]

The Romantic response to *Confessions* brought some derision from critics. Nietzsche, for instance, thought the long self-accusation over the pear theft bathetic: "Such tear-jerking phoniness." He had the same reaction to Augustine's lament over his friend's death in Book 4. "How psychologically phony—for example, when he relates the death of a friend with whom he made up one soul, and decided to live on, since this way his friend would not be entirely dead. What revolting pretentiousness."[4]

The Romantic Kierkegaard, on the other hand, had an Augustinian sense of cosmic drama played out within the soul (Harnack's comparison of *Confessions* with *Faust* is relevant here).[5] And the Romantic reaction to Augustine was still strong enough for William James, in his 1902 Gifford Lectures, to present him as a "classic sick soul," with a "divided mind," who needed to be "twice born."[6]

The Historicity Problem

The nineteenth century brought historiography to a new and deeper stage—away from the "conjectural" history of the eighteenth century, based on probability calculations, to the archival era, when the question was "what actually happened," as opposed to what various people said had happened. This "higher criticism" made its most dramatic impact on study of the Bible, where the chronology and authenticity of ancient accounts were questioned. It took a slightly longer time to raise questions about church history, but by 1888, two important challenges were issued to the historicity of *Confessions*. One was a lecture by the great church historian Adolf von Harnack, the other was an article by Gaston Boissier.[7] Both men pointed to the discrepancy between what Augustine wrote at the time of his baptism and his later account of it. In the Cassiciacum dialogues and early letters, Simplician and Mallius Theodore, with their Neoplatonism, were more important influences on him than Ambrose. These inconsistencies were further pressed by Louis Gourdon in 1900 and Prosper Alfaric in 1918.[8]

But the real explosion over historicity was a delayed one. It did not occur until 1950, when Pierre Courcelle asserted that the most famous episode in *Confessions*—the garden scene called a "conversion"—was wholly or largely fictional.[9] Courcelle also expanded on Boissier's and Alfaric's suggestions that Augustine had become more a Neoplatonist than an Orthodox Christian in Milan, but with Ambrose playing an important role in that intellectual development. Courcelle has mainly set the terms of debate over the accuracy of *Confessions*. Leo Ferrari in a flood of articles pushed even further the thesis that Augustine made up the whole garden story; while others have argued that Augustine, in retrospect, sees providential patterns not evident to him at the time. Ambrose and Monnica are later recognized as God's instruments in the prayerful meditation that is *Confessions*. It is the thesis of my book that the superimposition of Genesis patterns on the events of his life makes the question of literal historicity beside the point, since Augustine is not writing history or autobiography.

Freud Arrives

If the eighteenth century gave us a Romantic Augustine, and the nineteenth gave us a historically problematic one, the twentieth century gave us a subject for Freudian analysis. Psychobiography found *Confessions* irresistible. Augustine was given a mother fixation, an Oedipal complex, and a homosexual orientation. Psychiatrists have naturally worked these themes—Werner Achelis in 1921, Charles Kligerman in 1957, R. Braendle and W. Neidhart in 1984.[10] Some modern authors are obsessed with the idea that Augustine was obsessed with Monnica. But just as sex is surprisingly absent from Augustine's sermons and letters, his mother is absent from the mass of his writings, with the exception of the Cassiciacum dialogues, where she was a participant, and *Confessions*, which contains a funeral elegy for her.

Mothers play no important role in Augustine's vast writings. You would not know that from some modern treatments of Monnica. Arthur Darby Nock wrote that Augustine was "under the influence of her life and faith." [11] Muriel Spark called her a dominating, if not bullying, presence.[12] Rebecca West claimed of Monnica:

> She did not want her son to grow up. It was fortunate that in her religion she had a perfect and, indeed, noble instrument for obtaining her desire that he should not become a man. Very evidently, Christianity need not mean emasculation, but the long struggles of Augustine and Monica imply that in his case it did. . . . With her smooth competence she must have been able to make the Church a most alluring prospect.[13]

Jacques Derrida, speaking at the time of his own mother's death, said that the mother is at the center of Augustine's *Confessions*, as of his own *Circumfessions*.[14]

One test of the role of mothers in Augustine's thought is his lack of emphasis on the Virgin Mary. "He never dedicated a separate work to the subject and did not advocate a Marian devotion (*cultus*) in any of his collected works."[15] He did not believe in the Immaculate Conception (exempting Mary from original sin and the need for salvation), or in her bodily assumption (despite the African cult of martyrs' bodies). She was not a mediator between God and man—only Jesus can be that. She is not "the second Eve"—the Church is: "Adam and Eve were the parents of our death. Christ and the Church are the parents of our life."[16] Mary's faith is more stressed than her virginity—"She believed before she conceived" (*Fides in mente, Christus in vente*).[17] Augustine cites Matthew 12.50, "Whoever does the will of my Father in heaven, that person is my brother, my sister, my mother," to argue that "It counts for more, it is a far greater blessing, that she was a follower of Christ than that she was the mother of Christ."[18] "Mary is holy, Mary is blessed, but the Church is a better thing than Mary. Why? Because she is a part of the Church ... and the whole is better than the part."[19]

The Philosophers

The Romantic reading of Augustine often left out the last four books of *Confessions*; but modern philosophers have reversed that pattern, concentrating on the last four to the neglect of the first nine. Existentialists and phenomenologists have been sympathetic to Augustine's subjective treatment of memory and time in Books 10 and 11, while analytic philosophers, following Wittgenstein's criticisms, have thought Augustine unscientific. It was known that Augustine's treatment of time was a major influence on Martin Heidegger's *Sein und Zeit* (1927), but the extent of his indebtedness was confirmed when his 1924 lecture "The Concept of Time" and his 1921 lecture course "Augustine and Neoplatonism" were published in 1989 and 1995.[20] These works threw new light on his relationship with his predecessor Edmund Husserl and with his student Hannah Arendt (whose doctoral dissertation was on Augustine).[21] In the 1924 lecture, Heidegger describes time as the distinctly human (*Dasein*) running into the future to take possession of the past. He does this by meditating on Augustine's words at 11.36:

> So time is measured, my mind, in you. Raise no clamor against me—I mean against youself—out of your jostling reactions. I measure time in you, I tell you, because I measure the reactions that things caused in you by their passage, reactions that remain when the things that occasioned them have passed on. I measure such reactions when I measure time.[22]

Ludwig Wittgenstein debunked Augustine's view of time as illogical—one that cannot say he understands something until asked about it.[23] But Augustine was describing a psychological condition, not laying out a logical proposition. Wittgenstein also attacked Augustine's claim that he taught himself language.[24] But this is another example of people's problem when they read only *Confessions* and not Augustine's other works. Augustine's early dialogue *The Teacher* has a fuller and less vulnerable explanation of how children learn language. Wittgenstein does not deal with that text, the most relevant one. Noam Chomsky's writings on the innate aspects of language support Augustine's account of his own learning process.

Postmodern interpretations of Augustine have concentrated on *Confessions* alone. Jacques Derrida calls confession an opening of a wound and compares it to his own circumcision as a probing of identity and the past—hence his title *Circumfessions*.[25] Jean-François Lyotard's posthumous book *The Confession of Augustine* is made up of unfinished lecture notes and jottings on time. The three presents of Augustine—the presence of the past, the presence of the present, and the present of the future—are also seen as three absences, time always escaping from the effort to pin it down, always coming to consciousness too late (*sero*), as the identify being asserted also escapes from Augustine.[26]

It is remarkable, given the five million words of Augustine, that he does elude his commentators. In one way, we can know more about Augustine than of any other figure in Late Antiquity. In fact, with the exception of Cicero, we probably know more *about* him than about any classical figure. But even his most-read book is rarely read through with equal attention to all its parts. He was inventing a new form, and people try to read it as something other than the unique thing it is—as autobiography, or as treatise, or as an amalgam of different genres with different purposes. That has happened to other works that defy categorization. Virgil took the outward adventure stories of Homer and made them simultaneously an inward journey, a psychological adventure story, and an exploration of the meaning of empire, of its costs and its rewards. Dante took the cosmography of the theologians and made of it the soul's pilgrimage toward God. But people rarely complete these journeys. For every person who reads Dante's *Paradiso* there are perhaps twenty who read his *Inferno*. They want to linger with Paolo and Francesca rather than meet God with Beatrice. In the same way, people want to stay behind with Dido rather than journey on toward

Rome with Aeneas. That is why so few read about the Trinity in Books 11 through 13 of *Confessions*, even though that is the key to the whole book, the clue that we should always have been following. It should not be surprising that a long prayer should end in the presence of the God being prayed to.

CHAPTER 1 The Book's Birth

 1. Pierre-Marie Hombert, *Nouvelles recherches de chronologie augustinienne* (Institut d'études Augustiniennes, 2000), 9–23. Hombert thinks that *Confessions* was conceived as a unity and that Augustine just dawdled in completing it.

CHAPTER 2 The Book's Genre

 1. Charles Kligerman, "Psychoanalytic Study of the *Confessions* of St. Augustine," *Journal of the American Psychoanalytic Association* 5 (1957): 469ff.; R. Braendle and W. Neidhart, "Lebensgeschichte und Theologie," *Theologische Zeitschrift* 40 (1984): 157ff.

CHAPTER 5 The Book's "Conversion"

 1. Pierre Courcelle, *Recherches sur les "Confessions" de saint Augustin* (Boccard, 1950), 175–202.

2. Alexander Sizoo, *Vigiliae Christianae* 12 (1958): 104–6.

CHAPTER 6 The Book's Baptismal Days

1. See, for instance, Bernard Silka, Ralph W. Hood, Jr., and Richard L. Gorsuch, *The Psychology of Religion: An Empirical Approach* (Prentice-Hall, 1985), 199–224.
2. Augustine, *Happiness in This Life* 26.
3. Augustine, *Order in the Universe* 45.
4. Augustine, *Happiness in This Life* 10.
5. Ibid., 8. Monnica did not realize she was using one of Plotinus's arguments for the separability of mind from body: "You could list many worthy activities, theoretical and practical, which might as well not exist, so far as we are aware when we are thinking while doing them" (*The Nines* 1.4.10).
6. Augustine, *Order in the Universe* 10.
7. Brent D. Shaw, "The Family in Late Antiquity," *Past and Present* 115 (May 1987): 3–51.

CHAPTER 8 The Book's Culmination

1. Augustine, *First Meanings in Genesis* 1.21.
2. Augustine's treatise *De Genesi ad Litteram* should not, therefore, be translated (as it often is) *The Literal Sense of Genesis* but *First Meanings in Genesis*.
3. Augustine, *First Meanings in Genesis* 4.41.
4. Ibid., 9.32.
5. Ibid., 4.41–55.

6. The sources of the symbols in the Venice mosaics have been traced by Kurt Weitzmann, "The Genesis Mosaics of San Marco and the Cotton Genesis Miniatures," in Otto Demus, *The Mosaics of San Marco in Venice*, pt. 2, vol. 1 (University of Chicago Press, 1984), 105–42.

7. Augustine, *The Trinity* 10.18.

CHAPTER 9 The Book's Afterlife Early Reception, Later Neglect

1. Edward Gibbon, *The Decline and Fall of the Roman Empire*, ed. J. B. Bury (Methuen & Co., 1909), 3: 431,

2. Peter Brown, *The Body and Sexuality* (Columbia University Press, 1988), 416.

3. Augustine, *The City of God* 14.17.

4. Friedrich Nietzsche, *Briefwechsel* (Walter de Gruyter, 182), 3: p.34.

5. John A. Doody, "Kierkegaard," in *Augustine Through the Ages: An Encyclopedia,* ed. Alan A. Fitzgerald et al. (Eerdmans, 1999), 484–86.

6. William James, *The Varieties of Religious Experience* (Library of America, 1987), 159–61.

7. Adolf von Harnack, "Monasticism and *The Confessions* of Saint Augustine, trans. E. E. Kellett and F. H. Marseille (G. Putnam's Sons, 1910), and Gaston Boissier, "La conversion de saint Augustin," *Revue des deux mondes* 85 (1888).

8. Louis Gourdon, *Essai sur le conversion de Saint Augustin* (A. Coueslant, 1900), and Prosper

Alfaric, *L'evolution intellectuelle de saint Augustin* (E. Nourry, 1918).

9. Pierre Courcelle, *Recherches sur les "Confessions" de Saint-Augustin* (Boccard, 1950), 175–210.

10. Werner Achelis, *Die Deutung Augustins* (Kampmann, 1921); Charles Kligerman, "Psychoanalytic Study of the *Confessions* of St. Augustine, *Journal of the American Psychoanalytic Association* 5 (1957): 469ff.; R. Braendle and W. Neidhart, "Lebensgeschicte und Theologie," *Theologische Zeitschrift* 40 (1957): 157ff.

11. Arthur Daraby Nock, *Conversion: The Old and the New in Religion from Alexander the Great to Augustine of Hippo* (Oxford University Press, 1933), 264.

12. Muriel Spark, "St. Monica," *The Month* 17 (May 1957): 309–30.

13. Rebecca West, *St. Augustine* (Appleton & Co., 1933), 26–27.

14. Jacques Derrida, *Circumfessions*, trans. Geoffrey Bennington (University of Chicago Press, 1993), 205–9.

15. Daniel E. Doyle, "Mary, Mother of God," in Fitzgerald et al., *Augustine Through the Ages,* 542–45.

16. Augustine, Sermon 22.10.

17. Augustine, Sermon 196.1.

18. Augustine, Sermon 72A.7.

19. Ibid.

20. Martin Heidegger, *Der Begriff der Zeit* (Niemeyer, 1989); *Augustinus und der Neoplatonnismus*, in *Gesamtausgabe* 60 (Klostermann, 1995).

21. Edmund Husserl, *The Phenomenology of Internal Time-Consciousness*, trans. James Churchill (Indiana University Press, 1964); Hannah Arendt, *Love and Saint Augustine*, trans. Joanna Vecchiarelli Scott and Judith Stark (University of Chicago Press, 1996); Philippe Capelle, "Heidegger: Reader of Augustine," in *Augustine and Postmodernism*, ed. John D. Caputo and Michael J. Scanlon (Indiana University Press, 2005), 115–26.

22. Martin Heidegger, *The Concept of Time*, trans. William McNeill (Blackwell, 1992), 6.

23. Ludwig Wittgenstein, *Philosophical Investigations*, trans. Elizabeth Anscombe, 3rd ed. (Blackwell, 2001), 36–37.

24. Ibid., 2.3.

25. See note 14 above.

26. Jean-François Lyotard, *The Confession of Augustine*, trans. Richard Beardsworth (Stanford University Press, 2000).

BASIC READINGS

Augustine, *Confessions*, translated by Garry Wills (Penguin Books, 2006).

James O'Donnell, *Augustine 'Confessions'* Volumes I–III (Oxford University Press, 1992). The definitive text and commentary.

Peter Brown, *Augustine of Hippo*, new edition with epilogue (University of California Press, 2000). The definitive biography, by the founder of modern studies in Late Antiquity.

Allan D. Fizgerald et al. *Augustine Through the Ages: An Encyclopedia* (Eerdmans, 1999). A useful compendium of articles on all aspects of Augustinian studies, with guides to further reading on each one.

INDEX

Academic Skepticism, 50, 58–59

Achelis, Werner, 142

Acts of the Apostles (Paul), 65

Adam: and fig leaves, 24; sin of, 31–32

Adam's tree, 76

Adeodatus (son), 26–27, 37, 82, 95; and baptism, 83–84; death of, 85; and death of Monnica, 96; and *The Teacher,* 26–27

Against Academic Skeptics (Augustine), 81

Alfaric, Prosper, 141

Alypius, 14; addiction to blood sports, 63–64, 86; and baptism, 83–84; at Cassiciacum, 80; commitment to Christianity, 82; garden story, 68–77; and sex, 63; and truth of Christianity, 74; and virginity, 74; as witness, 73

Alypius tribute, and Paulinus, 85

Ambrose, 16, 20, 24; accused of fomenting disorder, 47–48; and affair of Victory's Altar, 42–46; and Alypius, 63; and baptism, 56–57, 84; coup against Valentinian II, 46; death of, 10, 13; and Faustus, 54–55; as God's instrument in *Confessions,* 141–42; as influence on Augustine, 141; and Neoplatonic approach to religion, 50; relationship with Augustine, 22; and relics, 49–50; sermons, 55; significance of, to Augustine, 94; and silent reading, 5; in Trier, 55–56; typological technique, 56

Ambrosian chant: basis for, 48

Anaximines, 94

angels, 123–24

Answer to Academic Skeptics (Augustine), 79

Anthony the Hermit, 66

Apologia (Plato), 20

Apologia pro Vita Sua (John Henry Newman), 20–21

Aquinas, Thomas, 136

Arendt, Hannah, 145
Arians, 47; and views on Trinity, 43–44
Aristotle, 122
asceticism, 59; fusion with enlightenment, 35
astrology, 34; and Manicheanism, 35, 110
Athanasius, 66
Augustine: and Academic Skepticism, 50; addiction to sex, 63, 138; and affair of Victory's Altar, 42–46; and baptism, 17–18, 56, 60–61, 83–84; and baths, 76; belief in miracles, 46–47; birth and infancy of, 26; as bishop, 18; as byword for libertine-rake glamorization, 137; at Cassiciacum, 56; and celibacy, 61–63; and child's voice, 72; consecration as bishop, 19; departure for Rome, 40; dialogues, 81–83; dictation practices, 1–2; disaffection with Faustus and Manicheanism, 39; as dramatist, 66; and fight against sexual addiction, 70–72; finding time for writing, 14–15; first impression of Ambrose, 43; first letter to St. Jerome, 3; flashy Latin style, 137; and garden scene, 76–77; garden story, 68–77; and homosexual orientation, 142; ill health, 14–15, 41; and Jewish Scriptures, 54–55; knowledge of Scripture, 7; and language acquisition, 28; last conversation with Monnica, 94; letter to Profuturus, 14–15; as Manichean, 18, 26; and miracle mongering, 49–50; and mother fixation, 142; and mother of Adeodatus, 33; and nakedness, 23–24; and Neoplatonists, 92; non-contact with Ambrose after leaving Milan, 51; and Oedipal complex, 142; as philosopher-bishop, 20; as poor sailor, 41; as prolific writer, 4; relationship with Ambrose, 22; relationship with children, 26; relationship with Monnica, 85–97; religious background of, 18–20; return to Hippo, 18; rhetorical studies, 35; as schoolteacher in Carthage, 38; sexual fantasies of, 23–25; siblings of, 22; significance of Ambrose to, 94; and Simplician, 51; sins plucking at, 73; study in Carthage, 33; and teaching of rhetoric from Aeneid, 43; and translation of Scripture, 7–8; unquiet manhood, 24; validity of consecration as bishop, 12; and Virgin Mary, 143–44; voyage to Rome, 41; writing career, 17; as young sex hound, 138
Augustine, Works: *Against Academic Skeptics,* 81; *Answer to Academic Skeptics,* 79; *The Beautiful and the Decorous* (lost), 17, 37; *The City of God,* 10, 37, 136, 138; *Dialogues with Myself (Soliloquia),* 21, 46, 61, 79, 81; *Explaining the Psalms,* 12; *First Meanings in Genesis,* 21, 122; *The Gift of Continuing Fidelity,* 134; *Happiness in This Life,* 52–53, 81, 92; *Let-*

ters, 7–8; *The Manicheans' Two Souls, 38; Music,* 18; *Order in the Universe,* 81; *Reconsiderations,* 54, 133; *The Teacher,* 26–27, 146; *Teaching Christian Faith,* 136; *The Trinity,* 10, 21, 127, 138

baptism, 60–61, 83–84; Augustine's reaction to, 84–85; bath and, 23–25; Marius Victorinus and, 64–65; waters of, 131
baptismal font of Milan, 85
bath *(thermae):* and baptism, 23–25; scene at Tagaste, 23–25
bath scene: modern psychiatric interpretation of, 23–25
Beautiful and the Decorous, The (lost, Augustine), 17, 37
Bergson, Henri, 100
Bible: Greek translation of (Septuagint), 7–8; King James English edition, 8; Latin translation of, from Hebrew, 7–8; study of, in ninetenth century, 140. *See also names of books*
"big bang" (spiritual), 123
Body and Society, The (Peter Brown), 59–60
Boissier, Gaston, 141
books: afterlife of (Nachleben), 15–16; making of, 3–4; structure of biography of a, 15
Botticelli, 1
Braendle, R., 142
Brown, Peter, 138; *The Body and Society,* 59–60

Caecilian, Bishop, 19
Caecilian Christianity, and Manicheanism, 35–36

Caecilianists, 19
Caelestius, 135
Cain and Abel, 36–37
Calvin, 136
Carpaccio, 1
Carthage, 19, 41, 113; Augustine in, 89; rhetorical study in, 35
Cassiciacum, 56; spiritual retreat at, 79–81
Cassiciacum dialogues, 92, 141; Monnica and, 142
Catiline, 30–31
celebrity conversions, 65
celibacy, 59, 61–63, 139
Chomsky, Noam, 28, 146
Christian-Eastern movement, 33
Cicero: on friendship, 31; *Hortensius,* 35, 60; *The Orator,* 7
Ciceronian purists, 137
Circumfessions (Jacques Derrida), 143
citations, difficulty in locating, 6–7
City of God: as opposed to City of Man, 37
City of God, The (Augustine), 37, 138; misreadings of, 136
City of Man: as opposed to City of God, 37
"Clothe yourself in Jesus Christ," 72, 76
codex, binding of, 4
Colet, John, 136
Confessions: Ambrose as God's instrument in, 141–42; Ambrose's opposition to Monnica's devotions, 45; Augustine's later comments on, 133–35; as autobiography, 22; biography of Alypius in, 14; Book 4, 96–97, 139–40; Book 6,14; Book 8, 78, 98; Book 9,14,

Confessions (cont.)
137; Book 10, 10–13, 98, 145;
Book 11, 114–20, 145; Book
12, 120–25; Book 13, 125;
Books 10 to 13, as later addi-
tions, 99; Books 11 to 13, 12–
13, 148; compared to *Divine
Comedy,* 22–23; compared to
Pilgrim's Progress, 22–23;
compared to Rousseau's *Confessions,* 22–23; composed as
whole or in parts, 10–13; conceived as a unity, 149n1; dating of, 9–13; death of, in Middle Ages, 16; as defence of
embattled figure, 20; dramatic technique in, 68; and
Genesis, 32, 114; genesis of,
1–16; historicity of, 50, 91,
141; as long prayer, 21; Monnica as God's instrument in,
141–42; obstetric record of,
13; as one-sided non-fiction
epistolary novel, 21; peccadillo of pears and pigs, 29–33;
psychobiography and, 142;
re-emergence in Romantic
era, 137; resurrection of, in
fourteenth century, 16; Romantic response to, 137–40;
special meaning imparted to,
13; tenor of language in, 9–10;
textual reinterpretation of, in
various centuries, 16; tribute
to Monnica, 14; written as deliberate whole, 13–15
Confiteor, 13, 100
conscience, examination of,
13, 106
continentia, 60
contraception, 26
conversion, 58–59, 78–79
conversion stories, 64–68

copies, need for multiple, 3
copying, process of, 2–3
Council of Nicaea, 20
Courcelle, Pierre, 72–75, 141
curiositas (transgressive knowledge), 110

Damasus I, Pope, 42; and
affair of Victory's Altar,
42–46
Dante, 25, 76, 147; *Divine
Comedy,* 22–23; *Paradiso,*
132
death, meditation on, in medieval cathedral, 13
Derrida, Jacques, 146; *Circumfessions,* 143
diabolical affliction, marks of,
24
Dialogues with Myself (*Soliloquia,* Augustine), 21, 46, 61,
79, 81
dictation practices, in ancient
world, 1–2
Diocletian, Emperor, 18
Divine Comedy (Dante), 22–23
doctrinal essence of Christianity,
74
Donatists, 12, 18–19
dry land, 131

Easter (386), and Portiana, 47
Enlightenment, 137
enlightenment, fusion with as-
ceticism, 35
Erasmus, Desiderius, 136–37
Eusebius, *History of the
Church,* 3
Everett, Edward, address at Get-
tysburg, 7
eversores ("subversives"), 33, 39
existentialists, 144–45
Ezekiel, 8; vision of, and scroll, 6

fall of humankind, re-enaction of, 33

fasting, 60

Faustus, 16, 38–39; Ambrose and, 54–55; and language acquisition, 39

Ferrari, Leo, 141

fig tree, in garden scene, 75–76

First Meanings in Genesis (Augustine), 21, 122

fish in waters, creation of, 131

food, 108–9

fountain of life, 131

Freudian analysis, 142

Galileans, 74

Garden of Eden, 90

Garden of Olives, 90

Garden of Philip, basilica at, 49

garden scene, 63, 68–77, 141; aftermath of, 78–80; fig tree in, 75–76; in Milan, 58; and sex, 59

Genesis, 12–13, 32, 37, 142; and Adam's tree, 76; Augustine's treatment of, 100; commentaries on, 31; in *Confessions,* 13, 114; exegetical exercise on opening of, 12–13; first covert reference to, 24; mysteries of, 99; speculative nature of Augustine's reading of, 125; verse 1, 122. *See also First Meanings in Genesis* (Augustine)

Gervasius, 49, 87

Gettysburg: Edward Everett address at, 7

Gibbon, Edward, 137

Gift of Continuing Fidelity, The (Augustine), 134

Gnosticism, 60

Gnostic sects, 33–34

God: as constant absence, 105–6; the Father, in *Confessions,* Book 11, 114–20; the Holy Spirit, in *Confessions,* Book 13, 125; as recipient of *Confessions,* 21–22; the Son, in *Confessions* Book 12, 120–25

God's robots, 134

Goethe, Johann Wolfgang von: *Faust,* 137; *Sorrows of Werther,* 137; *Wilhelm Meister's Apprenticeship,* 137

Gourdon, Louis, 141

Gozzoli, Benozzo, 1

Gratian, and affair of Victory's Altar, 42–46

gratuito malus, 30

"Great Sinner" myth, 137–40

Greek astronomy, 113–14

Greek *vs.* Latin, 28–29

Happiness in This Life (Augustine), 52–53, 81, 92

Harnack, Adolf von, 137, 140–41

hearing, sense of, 109

Heaven's heaven, 122–23, 131

Heidegger, Martin, *Sein und Zeit,* 145

Hierius, 37

Hippo, Africa, 4, 19; Augustine's return to, 18; and birth of *Confessions,* 15

historicity, problems of, 50, 91, 140–42

historiography, 140

Holy Spirit, as bond of love, 129

Hombert, Pierre-Marie, 149n1; dating of Psalm commentary, 12

homosexual orientation, 142

Hopkins, Gerard Manley, 105

Hortensius (Cicero), 35, 60

human free will, denial of, 134
human makeup, analogy to God in, 126–27
Husserl, Edmund, 145

Immaculate Conception, 143–44
ink, mixing of, 2
inquietum, 24
Isaiah, 131
Isidore of Seville, 4

James, William, 78, 140
Jefferson, Thomas, *Notes on the State of Virginia,* 7
Jerome, 137; and celibacy, 139; in court of Pope Damasus I, 42; and deception, 74; dictation practices, 2; and Latin translation of Scripture, 7–8
Jesus: at Mount of Olives, 76–77; and Nathaniel's thoughts, 72; three temptations of, 106–7 (*See also* urges of the eyes; urges of the flesh; worldly designs)
Jewish Bible, 113
Jewish Scriptures, 54–55
John (of Revelations), 8
John, Gospel of, 72; first letter of, 106
judgment, meditation on, in medieval cathedral, 13
Julian of Eclanum, 59, 135, 139
justification, doctrine of, 136
Justina, and affair of Victory's Altar, 42–46

Kierkegaard, Søren, 140
Kligerman, Dr. Charles, 23, 142

Lady Self-Control, 71, 73
language, human, divine mysteries cloaked in, 121

language acquisition, 26–27; and Faustus, 39; Noam Chomsky and, 28
Last Judgment, scenes of, 99–100
Latin *vs.* Greek, 28–29
lector, role of, 5
"Let there be light," 130
liberal arts, 18, 38
lights in the heavens, 131
Lincoln, Abraham, and King James English Bible, 8
literary industrial complex, ancient, 4
Luther, Martin, 136
Lyotard, Jean-François, *The Confessions of Augustine,* 146

Madauros, 28; Augustine in, 89
Mallius Theodore, 16, 22, 55, 92; biography of, 51–53; as influence on Augustine, 141; and Neoplatonist teachings, 50–51
Manicheanism, 18–19, 33–34; and astrology, 35; banned by Christian Roman Empire, 34; and Caecilian Christianity, 35–36; cosmology of, 38; rejection of Jewish Scripture, 33–34; two wills posited by, 69
Manicheans, 12, 38; Augustine as, 26; in Carthage, 33–34
Manicheans' Two Souls, The (Augustine), 38
Marcus Aurelius, 60; *To Myself (Meditations),* 21
Marius Victorinus, 50; and baptism, 64–65
Martial, 23
martyr relics, 46
Matthew, Gospel of, 144

Maximus: and affair of Victory's
    Altar, 42–46; move from
    Trier to Milan, 87
Memor, Bishop, 59
memory, 100–106, 126–28, 145;
    as act of self-destruction, 103;
    as analogy to Trinity, 127–29;
    capabilities of, in *Confessions*,
    7; as inner exploration, 102; as
    key to identity, 100; power of,
    in oral culture, 7; and time,
    117–19
mental ascent to God, 93
Milan, 18, 20, 22; baptismal font
    of, 85; garden scene in, 58
Milton, John, *Paradise Lost*, 32
Monica, Saint, 86
Monnica, 37, 82, 150n5; and
    Cassiciacum dialogues, 142;
    criticisms of, 86; death of,
    85–86; and drinking, 87–88,
    135–36; as God's instrument
    in *Confessions*, 141–42; last
    days, 94–97; and marriage
    arrangements, 63; at Milan,
    44–45; as model wife, 88–
    89; and mother of Adeoda-
    tus, 62; and Arthur Darby
    Nock, 143; as peacemaker in
    Tagaste, 89; and Portiana
    controversy, 48; relationship
    to Augustine, 85–97; as Saint
    Monica, 86; and Muriel
    Spark, 143; as supporter
    of Ambrose against Valen-
    tinian II, 45; and Rebecca
    West, 143
Moses, as author of Genesis,
    120
mother fixation, 142
motives, understanding of,
    29–31
Music (Augustine), 18

Nachleben, 15–16
naked body, physical inspection
    of *(scrutatio)*, 24
Nathaniel's thoughts, Jesus
    and, 72
Nathaniel's tree, 76
Navigius, 95
Neidhart, W., 142
Neoplatonism, 60; Ambrose
    and, 50; ascent to happiness,
    119; as influence on Augus-
    tine, 141; teachings of, 50–51
Neoplatonists, 58–59; Augustine
    and, 92
New Age spirituality, 33
Newman, John Henry,
    Apologia pro Vita Sua,
    20–21
Nietzsche, Friedrich, 139
Nock, Arthur Darby, 78; and
    Monnica, 143
nocturnal emission, 107–8

O'Donnell, James, 4, 17, 21, 50–
    51, 57, 99; on Augustine and
    Ambrose, 47; controversy
    with Courcelle, 74; expecta-
    tion of salacious content in
    Confessions, 137–38; and
    New Age spirituality, 33; and
    patterns of three, in *Confes-
    sions*, 13
Oedipal complex, 142
oral culture: in ancient world,
    4–6; and memory, 7
Orator, The (Cicero), and public
    speaking, 7
Order in the Universe (Augus-
    tine), 81
Origen, 3; and castration, 60
original sin, signs of, in infants,
    27–28
Ostia, 22, 85–86, 94–97

paganism, surviving vestiges of, in Rome, 42
papyrus, preparation of, 4. *See also* scrolls
Paradise Lost (Milton), 32
Paradiso (Dante), 132
parchment, preparation of, 4
Patrick, 89
Paul, 5, 78; Acts of the Apostles, 65; baptism of, 58; "Clothe yourself in Jesus Christ," 24; dictation practices, 2; dispute at Antioch, 74; Epistle to the Corinthians, 6; Epistle to the Romans, 3, 73; letters of, 72
Paulinus of Nola, 63; and Alypius tribute, 85
pears and pigs, peccadillo of, 29–33, 139
peer pressure, 29, 33
Pelagian heresy, 134
Pelagius, 59; response to *Confessions,* 134
pens, reed, preparation of, 2
Peter, and dispute at Antioch, 74
phenomenologists, 144–45
phrase salesman, trade of, 80
pigs and pears, peccadillo of, 29–33
Pilgrim's Progress, 22–23
Plato: *Apologia,* 20; *Phaedrus,* 5
Plotinus, 150n5
Pontician, and renunciation stories, 66
Portiana (basilica), controversy over, 47–49
principium, 121–22
Profuturus, 14–15
Protasius, 49, 87
Protestant Reformation, 136

Proust, Marcel, 100
Psalms, 9, 36; Ps. 4, 80, 137; Ps. 65, 131; Ps. 93, 131; Ps. 115, 122; Ps. 148, 122
psychiatric interpretations: and anachronism, 24–25; and bath scene, 23–25
psychobiography, and *Confessions,* 142
public baths, place of, in ancient life, 23

reading, in ancient world, 5–6
reason, abandonment of, and sexual orgasm, 60
Reconsiderations (Augustine), 54, 133
remembering forgetting, 105–6
Renaissance, 136
renunciation: act of, 64–65; stories of, 64–68
requiescat, 24
Revelation, scroll in, 6
ritual cleansing, *Confessions: Book 10* as act of, 99
Romanian, 40, 81; and Augustine's return to Tagaste, 35; patronage of, 33
Romans, Book of, 73
Rome, 22, 41; paganism in, 42
Rousseau, Jean-Jacques, 137; *Confessions,* 22–23

Sallust, 30–31
San Marco, basilica of (Venice), mosaics in, 124, 151n6
Scientist in the Crib, The, 28
scribes, prevalence of, in ancient world, 1
scripta continua, 5–6
Scripture, 20–22, 35, 59; Latin translation of, from Hebrew

(Jerome), 7–8; study of, 112;
understanding, 113–14
scrolls: papyrus, use of, 2; replication of, 2–3
scrutatio, 24
Septuagint, 7–8
Sergius Paul, 65
Seven Cardinal Virtues, as guide to spiritual danger, 106
Seven Deadly Sins, as guide to spiritual danger, 106
sexual addiction, fight against, 70–72
sexual dreams, complicity in, 107–8
sexual orgasm, and abandonment of reason, 60
sexual temptation, escape from, 79
Sicily, 41
sight, sense of, 109
Simplician, 16, 55; Augustine and, 51; as influence on Augustine, 141; and Neoplatonist teachings, 50–51; and renunciation stories, 64–65
Sizoo, Alexander, 75
smell, sense of, 109
Socrates, 5, 20
solitude, of reader and writer, 4–6
Spark, Muriel, 143
specific gravity, 130
spiritual psychodrama, 25
Stoicism, 60
Symeon Stylites, 59–60
Symmachus, and affair of Victory's Altar, 42–46

tablets (wax or wood), use of, 2
tachygrapher, 2

Tagaste, 85; Augustine's return to, 29, 35; scene in the baths of, 23–25
Teacher, The (Augustine), 146; Adeodatus and, 26–27
Teaching Christian Faith (Augustine), 136
Ten Commandments, as guide to spiritual danger, 106
Theodosius, 60; actions against Maximus, 87; and affair of Victory's Altar, 42–46; support for Valentinian II, 43
thermae. See bath *(thermae)*
time, 115–25, 145–47; and memory, 117–19
toothache, 80
Trinity: analogues to, 100–101, 127; in *Confessions,* Book 13, 125; mystery of, 13; perversion of values of, 107
Trinity, The (Augustine), 21, 127, 138
truth of Christianity, Alypius and, 74

understanding, as analogy to Trinity, 127–29
urges of the eyes, 110
urges of the flesh, 107–9

Valentinian II: and affair of Victory's Altar, 42–46; and Ambrose, 43
Valerius, as Bishop of Hippo, 19
Verecundus, 61–62
Victory's Altar, affair of, 42–46
Vindician, 35
Virgil, 147; lessons in, 81
virginity, Alypius and, 74
vocation stories, 64

West, Rebecca, 143
will: as analogy to Trinity, 127–29; damaged by sin, 69; theories of, 68–69
Wittgenstein, Ludwig, 145–46
world, creation of, 120–23
worldly designs, 110–11

writing: as musical score, 5; and oral culture, 4–6; process of, 2–3; without word-separation or punctuation, 5
writings, sacred, presence in *Confessions,* 8–9